Word Fact Finder

Terry O'Brien is an academician by vocation and a passionate quiz enthusiast by avocation. He has written and edited several bestselling books and series, including the Little Red Book series, the Fun Facts series, the Classic Tales for Children series, and the Fables from India series.

By the same author

Little Red Book Series

Little Red Book of Slang-Chat Room Slang
Little Red Book of English Vocabulary Today
Little Red Book of Grammar Made Easy
Little Red Book of English Proverbs
Little Red Book of Prepositions
Little Red Book of Idioms and Phrases
Little Red Book of Euphemisms
Little Red Book of Effective Speaking Skills
Little Red Book of Modern Writing Skills
Little Red Book of Verbal Phrases
Little Red Book of Synonyms
Little Red Book of Antonyms
Little Red Book of Common Errors
Little Red Book of Letter Writing
Little Red Book of Perfect Written English
Little Red Book of Essay Writing
Little Red Book of Word Power
Little Red Book of Spelling
Little Red Book of Language Checklist

A2Z Book Series

A2Z Quiz Book
A2Z Book of Word Origins

Others

The Book of Fun Facts
The Book of More Fun Facts
The Book of Firsts and Lasts
The Book of Virtues
The Book of Motivation
Read Write Right: Common Errors in English
The Students' Companion

WORD  FINDER

TERRY O' BRIEN

Published by
Rupa Publications India Pvt. Ltd 2014
7/16, Ansari Road, Daryaganj
New Delhi 110002

Sales Centres:

Allahabad Bengaluru Chennai
Hyderabad Jaipur Kathmandu
Kolkata Mumbai

Copyright © Terry O'Brien 2014

The views and opinions expressed in this book are the author's own and the facts are as reported by him/her which have been verified to the extent possible, and the publishers are not in any way liable for the same.

All rights reserved.
No part of this publication may be reproduced, transmitted, or stored in a retrieval system, in any form or by any means, electronic, mechanical, photocopying, recording or otherwise, without the prior permission of the publisher.

ISBN: 978-81-291-3536-0

First impression 2014

10 9 8 7 6 5 4 3 2 1

The moral right of the author has been asserted.

Printed by Thomson Press India Ltd, Faridabad.

This book is sold subject to the condition that it shall not, by way of trade or otherwise, be lent, resold, hired out, or otherwise circulated, without the publisher's prior consent, in any form of binding or cover other than that in which it is published.

INTRODUCTION

Where the referential meaning ends within the pages of a dictionary, the quest of *Word Fact Finder* begins—to take a closer look at the English language, especially at the subtle differences between words as they are used.

Indeed, words are a very powerful force. The power of words affects not only those to whom it is spoken but also those who speak them. Therefore, it is important to be impeccable with the words we choose; positive or negative, the effect of words can be profound.

Word Fact Finder gives us the nuances of words and usage. The exact word is what matters. Words help us realize our ambition and our dreams, and give us the ability to appreciate things in life. But it is not enough to look at a word as a stand-alone; each word lives in a world of other words. Use *Word Fact Finder* to know where each of them stand and how each is subtly different, and discover a whole new side of the English language!

Part I

A

ABUSE or MISUSE

Abuse is the more serious term, constantly appearing in phrases like *child abuse*. **To abuse** means 'to make bad use of.' As noun or verb it can describe the physical (usually sexual), verbal or psychological mistreatment of others. When applied to drink and drugs, the word suggests an excessive, uncontrolled intake of the substance in question.

To **misuse** is to 'use for the wrong purpose'.

ACCEPT or EXCEPT

To **accept** is to 'receive':
- ✓ I accepted my brother's kind offer of help.

The less common verb to **except** means to 'take out', to 'exclude':
- ✓ He was excepted from the criticism which the rest of the staff members earned. (Except is also a preposition meaning 'not including'.)

ACETIC or ASCETIC

Two words quite easily confused in their spelling. And, perhaps at some subconscious level, the vinegary sense of one suggests the self-punishing sense of the other!

Acetic defines an acid which is in a diluted form of vinegar:
- ✓ The first acetic acid known to man was vinegar.

The adjective **ascetic** means 'denying oneself bodily pleasure for moral or religious reasons'. Somebody who lives this lifestyle is an ascetic.
- ✓ Sadhus in India live an ascetic life.

ACQUIESCE, ASSENT or AGREE

These three words have different shades of meaning.

To **acquiesce** is to 'consent without showing opposition':
- ✓ He acquiesced in the plans of the trade transaction although he had no part in making them.

To **assent** means to 'comply', to 'agree to' (usually without much eagerness). Agree covers these two senses but also extends to more positive meanings: to 'be of one mind with', 'be compatible with'.

ACTIVE or PROACTIVE

The choice between this pair of closely connected words has more to do with fashion than meaning.
- ✓ There's something about proactive in the way my boss plans projects.

A few years ago **proactive** was a buzzword; it has come into official lingo.

This should not be used as a synonym for 'very active', which is sometimes how it's used (**'You may be active but I'm proactive'**), but in the sense of 'instigating change' or 'acting without being prompted'. The word is really the counterpart of 'reactive'.

ACTOR or ACTRESS

One of a group of word-pairs describing professions where the neutral form has traditionally been reserved for the male sex. The problem comes with the 'feminine' form of each pair.

The tendency is to avoid words that designate the sex of the person carrying out a particular job, thus 'firefighter' is preferred to 'fireman'. An **actor** describes a person who acts on stage, film or TV irrespective of sex.

(The difference between 'actor' and 'star' would make a subtle difference—not all actors have star quality but most stars refer to themselves as actors when they want to be taken seriously.)

Other art forms are also home to unisex terms like 'author', 'poet', 'sculptor'. There are feminine forms of some of these terms: **'authoress', 'poetess'**. The feminine form may sometimes be retained—waiter/waitress; steward/stewardess; headmaster/headmistress—although, as far as the last two are concerned, there is a preference now for the sexually unrevealing 'flight attendant', and 'principal' for the head of a school. Job advertisements at times do discriminate: 'waitpersons' or 'post persons'. One of the fields where the sex difference still holds is the host/hostess distinction. 'Host' can be used for either sex.

AD HOC or AD LIB

Both of these Latin expressions are concerned with things done at short notice, and are sometimes treated as though they are interchangeable. They're not.

Ad hoc means (organized) for a particular purpose rather than being permanent. Ad hoc arrangements tend to be makeshift:
- ✓ He is an ad hoc teacher.

Ad lib (from ad libitum—'at will') means 'spontaneous', 'unrehearsed'. It generally applies to off-the-cuff speakers, who will get a reputation for ad-libbing if they make a habit of it:
- ✓ On stage, he was an ad lib humorist.

ADOPTED or ADOPTIVE

Adopted applies to the person who is being adopted (or to the plan, suggestion, etc.)
- ✓ The adopted children were likely to go through great trouble because of the woman.

Adoptive describes those who are doing the adopting—this word can only be applied to those adopting children, not to the children themselves.

ADVERSE or AVERSE

Two adjectives with a one-letter difference; they both carry a general sense of 'against'.

The adjective **adverse** means opposing or 'unfavourable.'
- ✓ Adverse weather conditions delayed our journey.

Averse is very often coupled with 'not', as in:
- ✓ 'I'm not averse to your suggestion'.
- ✓ Averse means 'reluctant', 'unwilling'.

ADVICE or ADVISE

The spelling differs by one letter between the noun and verb forms. When it comes to **advice/advise,** mistakes like the following are quite usual:

You will be introduced to your boss who will give you all the advise [should be advice] you need.

Advice is the noun form and the one which should have been used in the example above, while **advise** is the verb:
- ✓ We received some good advice [noun]/He advised us well [verb] (But the person giving the advice is an adviser.)

AFFECT or EFFECT

These two words sound very similar and are frequently mixed up. To add to the confusion, the noun which relates to the main meaning of affect is effect.

As a verb **affect** means to 'have an impact on', 'make a difference to':
- ✓ Rohit's drinking affected his health more than his personality. (Independent)

Also, as a verb, affect has the less usual meaning of to 'put on', to 'pretend':

To **effect** is to 'bring about', to 'carry through':
- ✓ They effected the most changes almost overnight.

The noun which relates to the verb **affect** and has the same general sense of 'impact' is not, as one might expect, affect but **effect**:
- ✓ The harmful effects of cigarette smoking are now well established.

AFFLICT or INFLICT

These are two similar-sounding words, both suggesting suffering and punishment.

If a condition **afflicts** a person or animal it causes them 'trouble' or 'distress':
- ✓ Delhi Belly (diarrhea) is a more widespread problem, afflicting most international travellers to India.

To **inflict** is to 'impose something unpleasant on someone'. This word focuses more on the punishment, condition, etc.

AGGRAVATE and ANNOY

The primary meaning of **aggravate** is to 'make worse'.

By contrast, **annoy** often means 'irritate':
- ✓ She was annoyed by the frequent interruptions to her work.

ALIBI or EXCUSE

An **alibi**, more precise and forceful than an excuse, is a defence (often in court) that denotes one was 'elsewhere at the time' (this is its literal meaning from Latin).

An excuse is sometimes just an 'explanation'.
- ✓ Her excuse for being late was that there was a traffic jam.

ALLEVIATE or AMELIORATE

To **alleviate** is to 'make lighter'. It's generally applied to moods.

To **ameliorate** is to 'bring about an improvement'. The tendency is to use the word about physical conditions (illness, poverty, etc.).

ALLOT, A LOT or ALOT

Allot means to 'parcel out' (the noun is allotment). It has nothing to do with **a lot** (i.e. a 'large quantity'). But the real error comes when these last two words are written as one—'alot'. Alot is always wrong.

ALL RIGHT or ALRIGHT

Probably under the influence of words such as 'already' and 'altogether', there is a growing tendency to run together the two parts of all right.

Alright is especially common in informal contexts—'It'll be alright if you come'—but is regarded by what is probably a diminishing number as less correct than **all right**. It better be avoided in informal writing.

ALLUSION, ILLUSION or DELUSION

Allusion has a meaning distinct from that of the other two. An allusion is an 'indirect reference' and it's often found in discussion of music, films, and so on (where it indicates references to other bits of music, verse, etc.).

Illusion and **delusion** are both to do with a 'mistaken idea' or a 'false belief'.

A **delusion,** however, is not something that is easily driven away by argument or brutal fact, as it may be a sign of madness:
   ✓ He began to suffer from the delusion that he was the final authority.

ALTAR or ALTER

The **altar** (noun only) is the 'communion table' in church or a 'place for making sacrifices'. **Alter** (verb only) means to 'change' (noun: alteration).

ALTERNATE or ALTERNATIVE

There's a clear distinction between these two, but they both contain the ideas of 'otherness' and 'change' and are frequently confused.

Alternative can be used as a noun or adjective, and indicates that another thing is being offered.

Alternate is both adjective and verb. As an adjective, it means occurring by turns 'every other':
- ✓ We have holidays on alternate Saturdays.

As a verb, **alternate** means to 'shift from one thing to another and then back again':
- ✓ Her moods alternated between euphoria and gloom.

The adjectival form of alternate shouldn't be used as a substitute for alternative:

Note: The city was an alternate [should be alternative] target and was bombed two days earlier than planned. (This suggests that the city was bombed by turns with another target.)

Alternative also describes technology, medicine, comedy, etc. which is not mainstream.

ALTOGETHER or ALL TOGETHER

Like a number of words and phrases involving the prefix 'al-' and the complete word 'all'—'already/all ready', 'alright/all right'—these are sometimes confused, particularly because the two words run into one when spoken aloud.

Altogether (an adverb) means 'entirely', 'with everything included':
- ✓ The birthday girl was altogether delighted with her presents.
- ✓ The newly married couple made seven trips during the year altogether.

All together means occurring 'simultaneously' or 'in the same place'.

AMBIGUOUS or AMBIVALENT

Ambiguous is an adjective meaning 'unclear', 'of doubtful meaning'.
Being **ambivalent** involves a more thought-out position since it means 'being in two minds' or 'experiencing conflicting emotions about something'.
(The noun forms are ambiguity and ambivalence.)

AMEND or EMEND

To **amend** is to 'improve by changing or correcting'.
To **emend** means to 'make alterations in a written text'.

AMIABLE or AMICABLE

Amiable means 'friendly', 'likeable':
- ✓ He was popular for his easy-going and amiable manner.

Amicable means 'in a friendly spirit', and tends to be found in situations where differences of opinion have been resolved without a quarrel, or where bad relations might be expected:
- ✓ They had mutual and amicable divorce.

AMNESTY or MORATORIUM

An **amnesty** is a 'general pardon' or describes a 'period in which crimes can be admitted to without penalty':
- ✓ The President has the power of amnesty.

A **moratorium** describes a 'stretch of time when an activity is halted'. It is often applied to the suspension of debt payment.

AMONG, AMONGST or BETWEEN

There's no difference between **among** and **amongst,** although the first version of the word is more widely used. There's no great difference between **among** and **between**.

AMORAL or IMMORAL

Amoral means 'outside accepted systems of morality'. The word implies lack of the conception of right and wrong. Animals are amoral, for example.

Immoral means 'contrary to accepted standards of morality'. The word frequently has a sexual application.

ANNEX or ANNEXE

There's a difference between the noun and verb forms of this word, and it is easy to confuse the two.

To **annex** (pronounced with a stress on the second syllable) is to 'attach', 'take possession of'.

An **annexe** (with a final 'e' and pronounced with the stress more on the first syllable) is an 'extension', a 'building attached to a larger one.'

ANOINT or APPOINT

To **anoint** was originally to 'smear with oil as an act of consecration'.
To **appoint** is simply to 'select for a position':
   ✓ She was appointed managing director at a relatively early age.

ANTICIPATE or EXPECT

These two verbs are widely treated as if they were interchangeable but there is a useful difference in meaning between them.

To **anticipate** is not merely to believe that something will happen (i.e. expect), but to 'take some action to prevent or lessen the consequences of what will occur'. Where expect is largely passive:
   ✓ They're expecting it to rain tomorrow.

Anticipate has more active overtones:
   ✓ Anticipating rain, she took her umbrella with her.

ANXIETY or ANGST

Although **anxiety** has a specialist medical application (describing an aspect of depression) the general sense of the word is 'worry', a 'nagging concern.'

Angst (from the German) also means 'anxiety', but it has philosophical overtones suggesting troubled soul-searching. Angst is anxiety with attitude.

APOLOGIA or APOLOGY

Despite the look of the first word, it has almost nothing to do with saying sorry or expressing regret.

An **apologia** (pronounced with the stress on the long second 'o') is a 'formal statement in defence or justification of a particular position'.

An **apology** is an 'expression of sorrow or regret', sometimes on others' behalf but usually for oneself.

APPRAISE or APPRISE

The verb **appraise** means to 'sum up', to 'estimate the value or quality of' something or somebody.

(The noun is **appraisal**—a way in which employees are assessed by their bosses.)

To **apprise**—is to 'give notice to', 'tell'.

ARBITER, ARBITRATOR or MEDIATOR

These three terms, all describing people who assess situations and sort out problems, are sometimes used interchangeably but they have distinct shades of meaning.

An **arbiter** is an 'umpire', one who lays down the law or sets a standard of taste.

An **arbitrator** is 'someone brought in to settle a dispute'. This word, rather than arbiter, tends to be used in trade disputes and the law.

A **mediator** is an 'individual who acts as a go-between', sometimes when two or more parties are in disagreement but often simply to keep things running smoothly.

ARCHETYPE or STEREOTYPE

An **archetype** is the 'original model from which copies are produced'.

A **stereotype** is a 'clichéd image', 'something which conforms completely to a standard pattern', and there is usually a negative sense to the word.

ARDENT or ARDUOUS

Ardent means 'burning with enthusiasm'.
Arduous means 'difficult to achieve' or 'tough'.

AROMA or ODOUR

Two nouns meaning 'smell': but one is more positive than the other.
If there's a difference it is that **aroma** tends to be applied to pleasant scents, particularly from food or drink:
- ✓ I can still recall the delicious aroma of teas from around the world.

Odour is generally associated with the less attractive smells such as body odour.

AROUSE or ROUSE

To **arouse** is to 'excite', to 'provoke', and is usually applied to reactions (interest, concern) or feelings (suspicion, anger).

Arouse is also used of sexual responses, as is the associated noun, arousal.

To **rouse** is to 'awaken', to 'stir up' and generally takes a person or animal as its object:
- ✓ The church bells roused him from his sleep.

AS IF or LIKE

The use of **like** as a link-word (conjunction) instead of **as if** or **as though** is very frequent:
- ✓ She looked like she had some good news to tell. (rather than the more correct...as if she had...).

ASSUMPTION or PRESUMPTION

An **assumption** can be a 'supposition which isn't supported by evidence'; 'false' is the adjective often partnered with it and, even if it turns out to be correct, it has more the sense of a 'guess'.

A **presumption** has more the sense of a 'probability', i.e. it is more than guess work.

ASSURE, ENSURE or INSURE

These three verbs, all containing some idea of 'guarantee', are related but have different applications.

To **assure** is to 'guarantee', to 'give certainty to someone':
- ✓ They did their best to assure him that he was welcome.

To **ensure** is to 'make something safe or certain':
- ✓ Careful preparation helped to ensure the success of the student.

To **insure** is to 'protect oneself (financially) against loss or damage':
- ✓ We've insured the car.

AUGER or AUGUR

An **auger** (noun only) is an 'instrument for boring holes', usually in wood. An **augur** is a 'fortune-teller', the word deriving from the ancient Roman practice of telling the future through bird flights (which were seen as auguries).

AURAL or ORAL

Aural means 'of the ear'.
Oral means 'relating to the mouth'.

AVENGE or REVENGE

To **avenge** means to 'look for retribution' for a harm done not to the avenger but to somebody close to him/her.

To **revenge** is to 'harm in exchange for a wrong done to oneself'.

B

BAIL or BALE

Bail is a noun and verb with several meanings. An accused person will obtain bail, or be bailed, in court, i.e. 'gain release from custody before trial by providing some security' (usually financial) which will be forfeit if the defendant disappears. To bail also means to 'clear water out of' something, and to 'parachute out of an aircraft'. And finally, cricket stumps are topped by bails.

Bale can also be used as a verb in two of the senses above (baling water; baling out of a crashing aircraft). As a noun bale means a 'bundle' (a bale of cotton); as a verb, to 'do up in bundles' (baling hay).

BALMY or BARMY

Balmy (from balm, a healing ointment) means 'gentle', 'soothing'.

Barmy derives from barm, the froth on the head of fermenting liquor. So it means 'frothy' and therefore 'foolish', 'not right in the head'.

BENEFICENT, BENEFICIAL, BENEVOLENT or BENIGN

Beneficent means 'kind or charitable' and tends to describe people and their actions or outlook.

Beneficial can mean simply 'useful', as in 'a beneficial exchange of views', but its most usual context is probably to do with 'promoting health or well-being'.

Benign, with the sense of 'kindly', is more to do with attitude than action (a benign smile, a benign presence) and has a specialist sense in describing a 'non-cancerous' growth—the opposite of 'malign, malignant'.

BEREAVED or BEREFT

Bereaved means 'deprived of by death', and should be used only about those who were genuinely close to the dead person. **Bereft** (originally having the same meaning as bereaved) generally means 'deprived of something or somebody significant', without having a necessary reference to death.

BESIDE or BESIDES

These two words are often used as though they were completely interchangeable. They aren't.

Beside means 'next to' ('the table stood beside the window'). **Besides** means 'in addition to' ('besides the table, the room contained several chairs') and 'apart from' ('besides the table and chairs, the room was empty'). Besides, generally followed by a comma, also has the sense of 'moreover' ('Besides, there was nothing to be seen in the room').

BIANNUAL or BIENNIAL

Biannual means 'occurring twice a year'.

Biannual ought not to be used to mean 'occurring every two years.'

Biennial means 'occurring every two years' and describes festivals or conferences which conform to this pattern or, as a noun, it applies to a 'plant which flowers or fruits only in its second year'.

BIAS or PREJUDICE

Bias is a milder form of prejudice.

A **prejudice** is an 'already formed opinion or reaction', i.e. one which isn't reasoned but usually emotional or instinctive.

BIZARRE or BAZAAR

Bizarre means 'odd to the point of being fantastically strange'.
A **bazaar** is a 'market-place' but it carries exotic overtones of crowded muddle.

BLOND or BLONDE

Blond, meaning 'fair', 'light-coloured', applies almost exclusively to hair colour. Both noun and adjective take the final 'e' if the subject is female.
When the word is applied to a masculine subject it should, strictly speaking, be spelled without the 'e'.

BON VIVANT or BON VIVEUR

A **bon viveur** is a 'pleasure-lover', a 'man about town'.
The term **bon vivant** is used in France with the meaning of 'jovial'.

BORN or BORNE

Borne is the past participle form of the verb *to bear*. It is applied to the carrier.
  ✓ She had borne him four children.
Otherwise the correct form is **born**.

BREACH or BREECH

A **breach** is an 'opening'.
Breech describes the 'part of a gun behind the barrel' or the 'back or buttocks' (hence *breech delivery*, when the baby emerges buttocks- or feet-first).

BRIDAL or BRIDLE

Bridal means 'relating to a bride'. A **bridle** is 'part of a horse's headgear, and therefore 'anything which restrains'. A bridle path is one on which horses can be led or ridden.

BROACH or BROOCH

Broach, a verb, generally occurs in two contexts: to broach a topic, to 'introduce' it into conversation, often with the suggestion of difficulty.

Brooch, a noun, is an 'ornamental clasp'.

C

CALENDAR, CALENDER or COLANDER

A **calendar** is a 'table for telling the date' or simply a 'list'.

But **calender** is a word not in everyday use since it's restricted to a couple of specialist applications: a 'machine for rolling cloth or paper' or a 'member of a Persian religious sect'.

Neither word should be confused with **colander**, the 'kitchen container used for straining food'.

CALLOUS or CALLUS

Callous (which can be used to describe 'hardened' skin) is an adjective with the principal meaning of 'without feeling', or 'ruthless'.

Callus, which comes direct from Latin, is the noun for a 'patch of toughened skin'.

CAN or MAY

Can denotes ability:
- ✓ She can speak five languages.

but is often used in the sense of 'has permission':
- ✓ She's just been told she can come on the trip.

May indicates possibility:
- ✓ It may rain tomorrow.
- ✓ You may leave when the job's finished.

CANNON or CANON

A **cannon** is a 'large gun' or a 'type of shot in billiards'.

Canon has a variety of different applications: a 'priest attached to a cathedral'; a 'principle or rule' (as in 'accepted canons of decency'); the 'body of work attributed to a particular author' (the Shakespearean canon, for example, covers all those works considered to have been written by him and not attributable to another author). Canon also has an adjectival form, 'canonical'.

CANVAS or CANVASS

Canvas is 'material used for painting on, for making ship's sails', etc.; its plural form is 'canvases'.

To **canvass** (verb) is to 'gather support in a political setting' or simply to 'ascertain other people's views'.

Canvass also operates as a noun with the same sense of 'estimating numbers', 'gathering support for a vote'.

CAPITAL or CAPITOL

Capital has a range of meanings as a noun describing an 'important city' or 'seat of government', 'invested money', and generally 'stock'. As an adjective it means 'principal', 'connected to the head', 'involving the death penalty', etc. Capital comes from the word '*caput*' meaning head.

Capitol, on the other hand, has a very restricted meaning, originally describing just two imperial edifices: 'the temple to Jupiter in ancient Rome' (built on the Capitoline hill) and 'the area in Washington, D.C. where the Senate and Congress are sited', also on a hill. Capitol is slightly stressed on the last syllable.

CAPTIVATE or CAPTURE

To **captivate** is to 'fascinate', to 'enchant'.

To **capture** is to 'gain control of'. Although frequently used in a neutral sense ('to capture someone's attention') it also carries the meaning of to 'seize by force':

✓ The prisoner was captured after two days on the run.

CARAT or CARET

A **carat** is a 'unit of weight used for assessing precious stones and gold'.

The quality of gold in an alloy is measured in carats, each carat being one twenty-fourth of the total—hence 24-carat gold is pure gold. (The US spelling is usually *karat*.)

A **caret** is a symbol used in writing or proofreading showing where to insert something that has been left out.

CAVALRY or CALVARY

Cavalry is used to describe the 'troops who fought on horseback' and is now applied to the 'armoured and motorised part of an army'.

Calvary was the 'place near Jerusalem where Christ was crucified'.

CELIBATE or CHASTE

Celibate is an adjective or noun which describes someone 'unmarried'.

Chaste doesn't have to mean 'going without sex', although this is generally implied. It carries the sense of 'modest', 'restrained'.

CENSORED or CENSORIOUS

Both these words derive from **censor**, but the meaning of the second has more in common with the meaning of censure.

Censored describes a book, play, film, etc. from which material has been cut on grounds of taste, potential for causing offence and so on. The word also applies to the excluded material.

CENTENARY or CENTENNIAL

Centenary (noun and adjective) is a British English usage meaning a 'hundred-year anniversary'. **Centennial** is a rare adjective meaning 'happening once in a hundred years'.

CEREAL or SERIAL

Cereal is 'edible grain' (barley, wheat, etc.). As an adjective **serial** means 'occurring in a series' (serial number, serial killings); as a noun, it applies to the 'episodes in a continuing story' in a magazine, on TV etc. This word implies a stronger degree of continuity than series.

CEREMONIAL or CEREMONIOUS

Both adjectives derive from ceremony but they have different meanings and applications.
Ceremonial means 'with the proper ceremony or ritual'.
By contrast, **ceremonious** conveys a note of criticism and means 'over-concerned with ceremony' and therefore 'pompous'.

CHAFE or CHAFF

To **chafe**—pronounced with a long 'a'—is to 'fret or wear by rubbing'. It can have a physical application (chafed skin) or a mental one. If a person **chafes** (at, against or under something) it means that he/she is resentful and uncomfortable on account of some external circumstance.
Chaff is the husks of corn or other seed separated by threshing.

CHAOTIC or INCHOATE

Chaotic is obvious enough, having the meaning of 'very confused'.
Although something which is newly started may also be jumbled, even **chaotic**, there is a distinction between the two words and the writer ought to be certain of the sense in which he/she means it.
Inchoate means something that is not yet fully formed; rudimentary. It can also mean incoherent or confused.

CHILDISH or CHILDLIKE

Childish is used about adults in a critical sense, and describes behaviour which is 'non-adult', 'petulant', 'spoilt'.

Childlike is also applied to adults but this time often in approval, as it describes not so much behaviour as responses such as surprise and delight, or qualities like simplicity and trust—things that allegedly come more easily to children. Childlike is the opposite of 'worldly', 'cynical'.

CHRONIC or ACUTE

Chronic means 'long-lasting'. In itself a neutral word, it is almost always linked to some ongoing problem, as in 'chronic poverty', 'chronic back pain.'

Acute means 'sharp', 'urgent'—an acute illness is one which occurs suddenly and lasts a short time but may be life-threatening. Although a chronic condition will almost certainly be an unpleasant one, it does not necessarily endanger the life of the sufferer.

CLASSIC or CLASSICAL

Classic indicates that whatever is being described is an 'outstanding' example of its type or, at least, a 'highly representative' one: a book, film, song, dress, car etc. may be 'classic'.

As a plural noun, the term the classics generally has a bit of dignity and weight; it is applied to works of art (most frequently literature and music created before 1900) which have lasted and achieved the status of intellectual and cultural touchstones.

Classical is an adjective originally describing 'anything relating to the Roman and ancient Greek period'—history, literature, studies.

CLIENT or CUSTOMER

A **client** is (or sounds) slightly more upmarket than a customer, being a 'person who consults/employs a professional adviser'. Surgeons, lawyers and financial consultants have clients. A **customer** is 'someone who buys something', or a 'regular visitor to a shop'.

CLIMATIC or CLIMACTIC

Climatic is the adjective from 'climate':

✓ Climatic changes such as the earlier arrival of summer are a likely sign of global warming.

Climactic is the adjective from 'climax' and means 'culminating', 'most exciting'.

CLIMAX or CRESCENDO

Climax means 'culmination' and applies to the end-point and/or the most exciting moments in music, books, films and other forms of story-telling and sex. **Crescendo** used in its correct sense of meaning 'increasing loudness'.

More usual is the application of crescendo to mean 'climax' or 'highpoint'.

CODA or CODICIL

A **coda** is a musical term describing a 'passage which brings a piece to a satisfactory end'. So it comes to apply to anything which makes a 'fitting conclusion'.

A **codicil** is primarily an 'addition to a will'.

COLLUDE, CONNIVE or CONSPIRE

To **collude** is to 'conspire with', especially in fraud.

To **connive**, meaning to 'plot', is a less critical term. It can suggest turning a blind eye to another's unofficial or illicit activities, or a slightly underhand working together.

Conspire, once again to 'plot', is the strongest of these three terms and tends to be restricted to criminal or treasonous contexts.

COME or CUM-

Cum (the Latin for 'with') is used as a link word to show a double position or function: cook-cum-proprietor; cafe-cum-bar.

COMMON or MUTUAL

Common means 'shared', 'held jointly', as in common knowledge.
Mutual describes something which is 'reciprocated'.

COMPARE or CONTRAST

To **compare** is to 'put things side by side and look for similarities'.
To **contrast** is to 'look for differences'.

COMPLACENT or COMPLAISANT

Complacent means 'pleased', 'satisfied with a situation as it is'.
Complaisant means 'wanting to fall in with the wishes of others'.

COMPLEMENT or COMPLIMENT

As a noun **complement** is the 'number which will make complete' (as in a 'ship's complement') or an 'addition which makes for rightness or wholeness':
  ✓ For the British, chips are the right complement to fried fish.
Compliment, whether noun or verb, is 'praise':
  ✓ She complimented him on his skill in cooking.

COMPRISE or CONSIST

Both **comprise** and **consist** mean to 'include', to 'be formed of', but consist is always followed by 'of' or 'in':
  ✓ The New Testament consists of 27 books.
  ✓ The New Testament comprises 27 books.

CONFIDENT or CONFIDANT

Confident means 'self-assured', 'trusting'.
A **confidant** is a 'person in whom secrets are confided' and therefore a trusted friend.

CONGENIAL or GENIAL

Congenial and **genial** both carry the general sense of 'friendly', but

congenial tends to be applied to surroundings and atmospheres rather than to individuals. It also means 'sympathetic' or 'suitable'.
Genial is used about people and means 'pleasant', 'cheerful'.

CONSEQUENT or CONSEQUENTIAL

Consequent means simply 'following on from':
- ✓ The share price fell by some 12 per cent on the consequent scams.

Consequential can be used in the sense of 'resulting from' but its more usual meaning is 'significant'.

CONTAGIOUS or INFECTIOUS

A **contagious** condition is spread 'by direct contact' — all sexually transmitted diseases, for example, are contagious. An **infectious** condition (e.g. flu) is 'carried by microbes through air or water'. When applied metaphorically to something which is 'quickly spreading' — enthusiasm, panic — either word can be used.

CONTEMPTIBLE or CONTEMPTUOUS

Contemptible means despicable, 'worthy of contempt'.
Contemptuous describes a person 'who shows contempt', is 'scornful'.

CONTINUOUS or CONTINUAL

Continual also indicates something 'lasting over a period but with breaks or interruptions' and so means 'repeated'.
(The same distinction applies to the adverbs continuously and continually.)
Continuous means 'occurring without interruption':
- ✓ We had continuous rain for 24 hours.

CONTRADICTION or PARADOX

A **contradiction** is a 'denial' in speech or an 'inconsistency' in a view point.

If you contradict yourself you may be accused of fuzzy thinking, but to express a **paradox** suggests a more ingenious 'statement which appears to be contradictory but which, when examined more closely, contains some truth'. A contradiction usually arises by accident; a paradox is the deliberate formulation of an unusual point of view.

CORRESPONDENT or CO-RESPONDENT

A **correspondent** is a 'letter-writer' or a 'journalist with a particular field of expertise' (e.g. an arts correspondent or sports correspondent).

A **co-respondent** (sometimes spelled without a hyphen) is the 'man or woman cited in a divorce case as the third party'.

CORROSIVE or CORUSCATING

Corrosive means 'eating away', and so gradually destroying. It can be used literally or metaphorically.

Coruscating comes from 'coruscate' and means 'sparkling'. It may be used literally (e.g. of the effect of sunlight on water) but its most frequent application is metaphorical.

COUNCIL or COUNSEL

A **council** is an 'official group of people'; this is a noun only and is most often found in the context of local government.

Counsel is both a noun and a verb and carries the sense of 'advice or advising', often with a professional aspect to it.

Counsel also has the more specialised meaning of 'courtroom lawyer'.

CREDIBLE, CREDITABLE or CREDULOUS

Three words connected with ideas of belief and trust, but with quite different meanings.

Credible means 'believable':

✓ He had some extraordinary things to say but his quiet manner made them credible.

The adjective is very widely used now to suggest not so much that something exists (i.e. is not a fiction), but that it should be taken seriously, as in 'a credible fighting force'.

Creditable means 'worth praising', with the slight suggestion that whatever is to be praised has been achieved in difficult circumstances:

✓ Despite her injury, she put up a very creditable performance.

Credulous means 'easily deceived', too 'ready to accept whatever people say'.

CRITERION or CRITERIA

A **criterion** is a 'standard for judging' or a 'test', suggesting a level you must reach in order to qualify for something:

✓ The criterion for selection is specified.

The plural is criteria (never 'criterias'):

✓ They are based on criteria including innovation, financial soundness and long-term investment value.

CURRANT or CURRENT

As a noun a **current** is a 'stream of air or water'. As an adjective **current** means 'of the present time' (as in 'current affairs'). A **currant** is a 'small dried grape', a 'raisin'.

D

DECRY or DESCRY

Decry means to 'condemn'.

To **descry** is to 'find out something by looking'. It can be used of literal vision but is also used metaphorically for an attempt to peer into the future.

DE FACTO or DE JURE

This pair of Latin phrases is usually found together but they are opposites and shouldn't be confused. **De facto** means 'in fact', 'actually', and applies to the situation that exists without regard to what is rightful or what the law says about it. In contrast, **de jure** means 'by right', 'according to law'.

DEFECTIVE or DEFICIENT

Defective means 'faulty', 'badly made', 'not working to full effect', and can apply to body parts ('defective genes') as well as gadgets or merchandise.

Deficient means 'falling short', 'lacking in some way'.

DEFER or DELAY

Defer and **delay**, both meaning to 'put off', can be used almost interchangeably but there is also a difference of emphasis:
- ✓ 'Our visit was deferred' can mean not only that the visit was delayed but that it was put off until a later and specified time, often as a result of a conscious decision on our part.

Defer followed by 'to' also has the sense of 'submit', 'give way to':
- ✓ The board was compelled to defer to the wishes of the majority shareholders.

DEFINITE or DEFINITIVE

Definite means 'exact', 'not vague':
- ✓ Have you got any definite plans for the summer?

Definitive means 'decisive', 'final'.

Definitive also carries the sense of 'setting a standard'.

DEFUSE or DIFFUSE

Defuse can be used only as a verb and means, literally, to 'take the

fuse out' (of a bomb) or, figuratively, to 'bring calm into a tense situation':
- ✓ That's to say, making his life more comfortable, but also defusing his violent tendencies.

Diffuse as a verb means to 'scatter or spread through something or over a large area'.

DELIVERANCE or DELIVERY

Deliverance is a literary word meaning 'liberation', a setting free sometimes from a literal imprisonment but more often from a difficult or painful state of affairs. It is occasionally used as a euphemism for death.

Delivery also contains the idea of releasing or giving up, which turns into the notion of 'distribution'. Delivery is a bit of a buzzword at the moment, very popular in government handouts, company mission statements and other.

DEMUR or DEMURE

A verb and an adjective which look alike: They are not connected, although both have a suggestion of mildness about them. A fairly unusual word, **demur**—pronounced to rhyme with 'purr'—means to 'disagree with'. It does not suggest a violent objection, and is often found with 'not' as if to indicate that the speaker didn't feel strongly enough to disagree.

Demure—rhyming with 'pure'—is an adjective which means 'modest', with the suggestion of primness.

DEPENDANT or DEPENDENT

These two, one a noun, the other an adjective, comes in getting the ending right. Though spelled slightly differently they sound the same, hence the confusion.

Dependant is a noun only and describes 'someone who depends on another for support' (usually financial):
- ✓ She had four dependants, including her aged mother.

Dependent is an adjective meaning 'contingent', 'relying on':
- ✓ The college placement is dependent on his results.

DEPRECATE or DEPRECIATE

Two very similar words, both carrying the idea of 'running down, placing a low value on'.

Deprecate is more forceful than depreciate, and means to 'disapprove strongly of', to 'protest against'.

To **depreciate** is to 'go down in value':
- ✓ No car salesman is likely to depreciate his own products.

DERISIVE or DERISORY

Derisive means 'showing (humorous) contempt for'.

To describe something as **derisory** means that it is absurdly inadequate and can justifiably be treated with a dismissive laugh because it is 'worth deriding'.

DESERT or DESSERT

Desert is a 'dry sandy place' and, collectively, they—the Sahara, the Kalahari, etc.—are deserts.

An altogether different word, with the same spelling but a different pronunciation stressing the second syllable, is desert with the meaning of 'what one deserves'. This term, usually in the plural, has a negative ring. To get one's deserts, almost invariably just deserts, is to receive the unpleasant consequences of unpleasant actions.

Dessert—also pronounced with the stress on the second syllable—is the 'last course in a meal'.

DEVIANT or DEVIOUS

Deviant means 'departing from what is normal'. When used as a noun, the word almost always has a sexual application, a deviant being one step short of a 'pervert', at least in tabloid-speak.

Devious can mean 'winding' when describing such things as roads but a much more usual application is to people, where it means 'cunning'.

DIAGNOSIS or PROGNOSIS

Diagnosis can be used more generally, the original meaning of the word refers to the 'identification of a medical condition through its symptoms'.

The **prognosis** can only take place after the diagnosis since it is the 'forecast of the likely development' (of the disease or condition). Both words are often used outside a medical context, diagnosis to mean simply an 'analysis' and prognosis a 'prediction'.

DISCOMFIT or DISCOMFORT

These words have different roots in French and Latin, but they look alike and one often leads to another — if you're discomfited you'll probably feel some mental or physical discomfort as well. So it's quite hard to draw a line between them.

Discomfit (verb) is to 'disconcert', to 'embarrass', with the sense of being put on the spot.

(The associated noun is discomfiture.)

As a verb **discomfort** literally means to 'deprive of comfort', though in practice it is used in the same meaning as discomfit.

DISCREET or DISCRETE

These two words, originally derived from the same Latin word, are pronounced identically and also share the idea of 'keeping apart'.

But they have acquired quite different meanings.

Discreet is used almost always in the sense of 'being able to keep secrets or confidences' and therefore 'careful or tactful'.

The frequent confusion between these two may be made worse by the fact that the noun from discreet, **'discretion'**, looks uncommonly as if it's derived from discrete.

DISCRIMINATING or DISCRIMINATORY

Both of these words derive from **discriminate**, but the meaning of one is positive, the other negative.

As an adjective, **discriminating** is usually complimentary since it describes a person who is capable of 'showing good judgement' (often in relation to food and drink).

Discriminatory is generally negative since it carries the sense of 'prejudiced' (because a particular group is being picked out or discriminated against on grounds of race, gender, etc.)

DISINTERESTED or UNINTERESTED

Two words which sound similar and which everyday use has made into equivalents. But precise definitions and careful usage say otherwise.

To take the one with the obvious meaning first: **uninterested** means 'bored by', 'not attracted to':
- ✓ Few newspaper readers are uninterested in the private lives of public figures.

The original meaning of **disinterested** is 'neutral', 'impartial'. Correctly, this is the sense in which it's used here:
- ✓ Politicians seem to be disinterested public servants.

DISTIL or INSTIL

Two words, with identical endings and with vague 'chemical' overtones, whose meanings may sometimes be confused.

To **distil** is to 'produce in concentrated form'. The word describes a chemical process for producing spirits, perfumes, etc. but is frequently applied to any attempt to reach the essence of a situation.

To **instil** is to 'introduce slowly or drop by drop'.

DISTINCT, DISTINCTIVE or DISTINGUISHED

These adjectives, containing the idea of something 'standing out', tend to run into one another but they have separate functions.

Distinct means 'standing out', 'noticeable':
- ✓ There's a distinct smell of gas in the kitchen.

To describe something as **distinctive** suggests that it is 'typical or characteristic' of a person or place.

Distinguished means 'eminent', 'worthy of respect':
- ✓ After a distinguished career as a diplomat, he retired to write novels.

DOMINANT or DOMINEERING

Both of these similar-sounding words are to do with control but the first can be more or less neutral while the second always implies a criticism.

Dominant is 'leading', 'commanding', and can be applied to people, countries, styles, etc.

Domineering, almost always used about individuals, means 'overbearing', 'bullying'.

DOWNSTAGE or UPSTAGE

Downstage describes the 'area of the stage closest to the audience' while **upstage** is the 'area farthest away from the audience'.

To **upstage** someone, inside or outside the theatre, is to 'draw attention away from that person to oneself' (since an actor moving upstage may force the other actors to turn towards him, so putting their backs to the audience).

DRAFT or DRAUGHT

These words are very easily confused. They are pronounced the same, and both are connected to different senses of 'draw'.

Draft has the sense of 'something drawn'. As a noun it is a 'first version' of something like a plan or document, and as a verb it means to 'produce a rough, early version':
- ✓ He drafted the outline of his speech on the back of an envelope.

By contrast, a **draughtsman** is 'someone who works with designs or pictures'. The word **draught** is more concerned with the 'act of drawing'.

DUAL or DUEL

Two identically pronounced words which are quite easily confused, perhaps suggested by the idea of the 'two' sides involved in a duel.

Dual is an adjective meaning 'twofold': **dual** control, a dual personality:
- ✓ The briefcase, however, serves a dual purpose. It holds documents.

Duel is a noun or verb indicating an 'arranged fight between two individuals'.

DUE TO or OWING TO

Due to, meaning 'on account of', should be used only in an adjectival sense, so that it is actually qualifying a noun:
- ✓ The outbreak of food poisoning was probably due to the stale chicken.

The different applications of **due to/owing to** are not observed by many people.

E

EATABLE or EDIBLE

If something is **edible** then it is 'safe to eat', that is, it won't poison you:
- ✓ Many kinds of mushroom are not edible.

Eatable then it is 'fit to eat', even quite good—but the word does not convey much enthusiasm and you wouldn't use it as a compliment on someone's cooking.

ECONOMIC or ECONOMICAL

These two terms are frequently used as if they amounted to the same thing but there is a gap between their meanings.

Economic means 'relating to the economy', and can be used on several levels from the global or the national down to the personal.

Economical is an altogether more homely term, and when applied to an individual means 'careful with money'. When used about products it suggests that the consumer is getting value for money:
- ✓ This is an economical car: it averages 26 km per litre.

Economical can also suggest 'sparing', 'small in quantity' (an economical portion).

EERIE or EYRIE

Any confusion between these two arises because of uncertainty over their spelling rather than meaning.

The adjective **eerie** (sometimes eery) describes something which is 'strange', 'unsettling'. The word can have supernatural overtones but it generally seems to be used as a synonym for 'weird'.

An **eyrie**—which has variant spellings such as aerie—is the 'nest of an eagle' (or any bird of prey) but is more commonly used to describe 'any high and secure place'.

EFFECTIVE, EFFECTUAL or EFFICACIOUS

These words are very close—all having the sense of 'producing a result'—but they appear in slightly different contexts.

Effective tends to be used of people and things in the sense of 'having an impact', 'producing the desired result':
- ✓ Cigarette companies recently agreed to put more effective warnings on the packets.

Effectual is a much less usual word meaning essentially the same (and more frequently found in its negative form of ineffectual):
- ✓ The new warnings on tobacco products were effectual in reducing sales.

Efficacious also means 'capable of producing the intended result', but its use is almost entirely confined to medicines and remedies.

E.G. or I.E

The common abbreviations e.g. and i.e. (almost always appearing in lower case, and sometimes without full stops) are short for Latin phrases and are occasionally confused, through a misunderstanding of their individual functions.

The abbreviation **e.g.** (exempli gratia—'for example') introduces an example, one or two out of several.

In contrast **i.e.** (ildest—'that is') introduces an explanation or amplification of a previous statement:
- ✓ The President is the head i.e. the supreme commander.

ELDER or OLDER

People sense vaguely that there is some difference between these almost identical terms but are not sure what it is.

Of these two adjectives in the comparative form (the superlatives are eldest and oldest), **older** can be used in almost any context (an older person, an older car) while **elder** should be restricted to people, generally within a family framework (my elder sister). Elder also has the noun sense of 'someone who should be looked up to', on account of their years of experience, as in 'elders and betters'.

ELECTRIC, ELECTRICAL or ELECTRIFYING

All these terms derive from **'electricity'** but **electric** is used in a figurative sense to mean 'exciting' or 'startling' (an electric performance; an electric intervention in a debate) as well as in its literal application (electric light). **Electrical** simply means 'related to electricity' and is applied to supplies, faults, etc. (an electrical breakdown). The adjective **electrifying** is almost always used in the figurative sense of electric but carries an even stronger charge: 'astonishing'.

ELEGY or EULOGY

Two words that sound similar and which, in their origins, describe speeches or poems delivered on significant occasions.

An **elegy** was originally a 'song or poem of mourning'.

A **eulogy** can also be delivered at a funeral since it means a 'speech of praise', but it is frequently found in lighter contexts.

(The associated adjectives are elegiac—often employed to describe pictures, music, moods, etc., and meaning no more than 'pleasantly sad'—and eulogistic.)

ELICIT or ILLICIT

These words may be confused because they sound almost identical but in fact they have nothing to do with each other.

The verb **elicit** means to 'evoke' or 'draw out'.

The adjective **illicit** means 'not allowed', 'unlawful'.

ELOQUENCE or LOQUACITY

Each of these terms is connected to speech, one in a positive way, the other negative.

Eloquence is 'persuasive, flowing speech'.

Loquacity is 'talkativeness'. It tends to be used in a pejorative sense.

(The related adjectives are loquacious and eloquent. This second word can apply to other things apart from speech—a gesture can be eloquent [i.e. 'expressive'].)

EMINENT, IMMINENT or IMMANENT

The first two words are close in pronunciation, the last two even more so. The first carries the idea of importance, the second implies urgency. The last word is quite rare but is sometimes confused with the second.

Eminent means 'conspicuous', 'distinguished', and is usually applied to people.

The two words should not be confused.

Immanent is a fairly rare adjective with a specialist religious philosophical meaning of 'pervading', 'inherent'.

(The noun forms are eminence, imminence and immanence, respectively.)

EMOTIONAL or EMOTIVE

Both words are obviously connected to emotion, but have different applications.

Emotional tends to be used in the sense of 'excitable' or 'moody'. The word sometimes has a slightly critical edge to it.

Emotive means 'intended to stir the emotions'. It's usually applied to language and sometimes to images which set out to manipulate an audience by triggering certain responses:

✓ It was a highly emotive advertisement.

EMPATHY or SYMPATHY

Both nouns are to do with feeling. However they have fairly different applications which are worth preserving.

Empathy is 'imaginative identification with someone else' and his or her situation, whether that situation is a good or bad one.

Sympathy also involves the attempt to see things from the perspective of another person and carries the additional sense of 'compassion'.

(The related verbs are empathize and sympathize.)

EMULATE or IMITATE

Both of these terms are to do with 'copying' and are sometimes used interchangeably. But their associations are quite different.

To **emulate** is to **'imitate'** but it carries more positive overtones than the second word because the idea of rivalry is often involved rather than mere copying. Therefore to emulate is also to 'try to equal or outdo'.

To **imitate** is simply to 'copy'. The word frequently has negative associations—imitations are much more often described as poor than good.

ENDEMIC, EPIDEMIC or PANDEMIC

Three terms which are widely linked to outbreaks (of disease) and their spread. The differences between them are sometimes blurred.

Endemic, an adjective, means 'widely found among a certain group or in a certain area', and although often referring to disease it can extend to other topics.

Epidemic is a noun or adjective describing an 'outbreak'—usually of a disease (though one could talk of 'an epidemic of panic'). A characteristic of an epidemic is that it is relatively short-lived, unlike something endemic, which is likely to be there for good.

Pandemic is generally used to describe a disease prevalent over a whole country or the world.

ENORMITY or ENORMOUSNESS

Two words both deriving from enormous and suggesting size,—although the principal meaning of the first word is connected to crimes of great magnitude. (The Latin root of enormous indicates something which has deviated from the rule or norm.)

The first word in this pair is definitely the more widely used of the two, whatever the context. Strictly speaking, there is a distinction, since the noun enormity characterizes 'extreme wickedness' or an 'outrage':

✓ The enormity of the dictator's crimes had been exposed.

ENQUIRY or INQUIRY

The different spellings of this word may be appropriate in particular contexts.

Inquiry tends to be used for an official investigation, where the word is usually capitalized, but the general preference is to use the other spelling in such contexts as 'enquiries welcomed'.

ENVELOP or ENVELOPE

To **envelop** is a verb meaning to 'cover' or 'wrap round'. It is not spelled with an 'e' at the end, and the stress falls in the middle of the word:

- ✓ Whatever the reason, it's become the second controversy to envelop her this year.

Envelope, with the stress falling on the beginning of the word, is a noun only and describes the 'thing which does the covering':

- ✓ He had to nerve himself to open the envelope from the Income Tax Department.

EQUABLE or EQUITABLE

Both of these adjectives contain ideas of balance and evenness, but they are found in different areas.

The adjective **equable** means 'even', 'without extremes'. Frequently applied to the weather, where it means much the same as 'temperate', it also describes character:

- ✓ He had such an equable temperament that it was impossible to pick a quarrel or an argument with him.

Equitable means 'just', 'following the principles of fairness'.

EROTIC or PORNOGRAPHIC

This isn't a confusion so much as a matter of definition or rather a question of point of view since the definition of both words is essentially 'arousing sexual desire'. **Pornographic** carries the additional sense 'obscene'. But the words are constantly changing in this field, and what was yesterday's pornography becomes today's **eroticism**.

ESCAPEE, ESCAPER, ESCAPIST or ESCAPOLOGIST

The four words characterise the individual who seeks to get out of somewhere uncomfortable or confining, but each in a different context.

An **escapee** is 'one who escapes'. The word almost always has a literal application to describe the person who gets out of a jail. An alternative form is escaper.

An **escapist** is a 'person who is looking to escape from reality'. Someone who gravitates towards escapist material all the time may not be in a healthy state of mind:

✓ He argues that the flood of books about fairies and angels is a symptom of escapist despair by people.

An **escapologist** is a 'person who repeatedly gets out of tricky situations'.

(The related abstract nouns are escapism and escapology.)

ESPECIAL or SPECIAL

The adjectives **especial** and **special**, and the adverb forms (especially, specially), are used almost interchangeably although there is a useful distinction between them.

Especial and especially, meaning 'principal', 'very much', intensify whatever word they are linked with: an especial friend; an especially happy day.

Special is very often used in the sense of especial (a special friend, occasion, etc.) but it carries the additional sense of 'specific' or 'confined to a particular subject':

✓ I had a special reason for wanting to see you today.

Special can also be a noun: today's specials (on a menu).

ESTIMATE or GUESSTIMATE

An **estimate** is a 'rough calculation' or an 'attempt to judge the worth of anything'. A **guesstimate** is supposedly better than a 'guess' but less accurate than an 'estimate'.

EUPHEMISM or EUPHUISM

A **euphemism** is a 'word or phrase which expresses a potentially offensive fact or truth in a more palatable way'—and that's an elaborate definition for an activity which all of us practise every day. Euphemisms tend to cluster around the embarrassing or threatening aspects of life: sex, death, bodily functions ('sleep with', 'pass on', 'spend a penny'). More often, however, a euphemism is designed to blur the truth and can come close to being a lie.

By contrast, **euphuism,** sometimes used in error for euphemism, has a very restricted application since it defines a 'high-flown, extravagant style of writing' which was in vogue at the end of the 16th century.

EVERY DAY or EVERYDAY

These two are not identical and the distinction between them—one which is plainer in writing than in speech—should be kept.

Every day means just that, 'occurring daily':
- ✓ Looking back, it seemed as though the sun shone every day that summer.

Everyday (one word) means 'ordinary'—since something that happens every day soon becomes usual:
- ✓ The benefits of the everyday use of electricity is calculated.

EVERY ONE or EVERYONE

Every one is chiefly used of things:
- ✓ Dozens of used cars—every one a bargain!

Everyone is only used of people:

✓ Everyone was shocked by the news.

Every one can be used of people in a more emphatic or specific context:
  ✓ There were quite a few people in the room and every one was shocked by the news.

EVIDENCE or EVINCE

Two similar-sounding words which involve ideas of displaying or proving.

Evidence is mainly found in its noun use (the evidence in the case) but it can also be used as a verb with the sense of to 'make evident', to 'show':
  ✓ Some people don't like—all right, I don't like—this verb use of evidence. It sounds awkward and a simple word like 'show' will do a better job.

Evince means to 'show clearly', and is used of people rather than figures, data, etc.:
  ✓ He never evinced much interest in investment or business transactions.
  ✓ It had been a poor year for the company, as evidenced by the figures.

EXALTED or EXULTANT

A similar look to these two words, together with the idea of being at a kind of peak, may cause confusion.

Exalted (adjective) means 'high', 'dignified':
  ✓ Despite his exalted position, the President never lost touch with his roots.

Exultant (adjective) means 'triumphant'.

(The associated verbs are exalt and exult, while the noun forms are exaltation and exultation.)

EXCEPTIONAL or EXCEPTIONABLE

Exceptional means 'outstanding', 'excluded from the normal run of things':
- ✓ That summer was exceptional for its low rainfall.

Exceptionable means 'objectionable' (i.e. it describes something to which exception could be taken).

EXHAUSTED, EXHAUSTING or EXHAUSTIVE

Exhausted is simply 'very tired':
- ✓ Working for six months without a break left her totally exhausted.

Exhausting means 'very tiring':
- ✓ She found it exhausting to go for so long without a holiday.

Exhaustive means 'very thorough':
- ✓ When she came back she gave us an exhaustive account of her holidays.

EXHIBITER, EXHIBITIONER or EXHIBITIONIST

The term for a person who shows pictures, works, etc. at art exhibitions is an **exhibiter**. An **exhibitioner** is a 'university student awarded an exhibition' (i.e. a grant of money, usually made in recognition of academic achievement—this is an older and specialist meaning of exhibition). An **exhibitionist** is a 'person who likes showing off'. It also describes those people who expose themselves sexually in public.

EXHORT or EXTORT

Two words carry overtones of force.

To **exhort** is to 'encourage' or 'urge' and there is usually a faintly bullying overtone to the word.

To **extort** is to 'obtain something (usually money) by violence or the threat of it':
- ✓ The protection gang extorted money from half the discotheque in the city.

EXPLICIT or IMPLICIT

These adjectives are both applied to the meaning of something but in opposite senses.

The notice gave an **explicit** warning that shoplifters would be prosecuted. (Explicit is also the shorthand term for sexually frank language or action in the media. As such, it can operate as a warning. **Implicit** means 'suggested', 'not openly stated'.)

(Implicit also carries the sense of 'absolute', 'unquestioning': implicit trust.)

Explicit is 'frank', 'clear'.

EXTEMPORE or IMPROMPTU

Two words from Latin which are frequently used interchangeably although there are subtle differences of emphasis and application between them.

Extempore describes a speech, performance, etc. which is done 'off the cuff', 'without the help of notes' but not necessarily without any preparation.

Impromptu also applies to performances with the sense of 'unprepared', but it carries the additional meaning of 'makeshift' and can describe arrangements, structures and so on.

F

FACTIOUS or FRACTIOUS

These words not only look very similar but both contain the idea of 'troublesome'.

Factious—from 'faction', describing a small group (usually within a larger one) that has its own agenda—means 'inclined to form factions', 'trouble-seeking'.

Fractious means 'quarrelsome'. The word is generally applied to children. In some ways it's the junior version of factious:

✓ When the children get back from an outing, tired, fractious and hungry, it is essential to remove them to a safe place while you cook lunch.

FAINT or FEINT

As a verb **faint** means to 'lose consciousness briefly'; as an adjective it means 'not distinct', 'weak'. The word shouldn't be confused with **feint** (noun and verb) which describes a 'deceptive move made during a fight/battle to trick one's opponent'—usually to conceal the direction from which the real blow is coming.

FAIR or FARE

This is a pair of confusables, like 'bail/bale', with a raft of meanings attached.

Fair as a noun describes a 'market for business or pleasure'(antiques fair, tradefair, funfair). As an adjective, **fair** has a range of meanings from 'bright' (a fair day) to 'just' (a fair exchange) to the very English 'not bad' (fair marks). As a verb **fare** means to 'travel' or 'get on'—not much found now except in slightly quaint expressions like 'How are you faring?' As a noun a fare is the 'price of a journey' (train fare) or 'food/provisions', although this second sense seems restricted to supermarket advertising and the hospitality industry.

FANCIFUL, IMAGINARY or IMAGINATIVE

Three words associated with the imagination but with widely differing meanings.

'**Fancy**' in its old sense is connected to the 'imagination', it was regarded as a bit wilder and more frivolous.

This historical sense has pretty well disappeared but the adjective **fanciful** occupies ground somewhere between imaginative and silly; best defined perhaps as 'unrealistic'.

Imaginary means 'having no basis in reality', 'illusory'.

FARTHER or FURTHER

Farther means the same as **further**, and is preferred by some people when physical distance is the topic because it looks as though it is the comparative form of 'far':
- ✓ We overtook them a few miles farther on.
- ✓ Inflation rose further than expected last month.

FAUN or FAWN

Faun has only one meaning: it describes a 'mythological creature with a man's body and a goat's legs, horns and a tail'. It—or he—should not be confused with fawn, a 'young deer', even though in a sense both fauns and fawns are woodland creatures.

Fawn is also a colour ('yellowish-brown') and, as a verb followed by 'over', means to 'flatter or show affection'—always used pejoratively.

FAZE or PHASE

To **faze** (it only appears as a verb and in the participle form fazed) is to 'shake up', to 'worry'.

Phase is a noun and a verb. As a noun, it describes a 'stage in the development of a person, organization, etc.':
- ✓ Most teenagers go through a phase when they find their parents irritating.

As a verb, phase is usually coupled with 'in' or 'out', and describes a slow process in which something new appears or something old vanishes.

FEMININE, EFFEMINATE or EFFETE

Feminine means 'characteristic of women' and although used principally of women it can describe an attribute which a man might have: a feminine voice; a feminine sensitivity. **Effeminate,**

only used of men, means 'woman-like' and so 'unmanly'—it's a pejorative term:
- ✓ He is quite effeminate in his ways.

Effete has nothing to do with effeminate but, by a rather complicated process, moves from meaning 'worn out' (originally through childbirth) to 'barren' to 'degenerate'. In fact, the usual application of the word means something between 'useless' and 'frivolous'.

FERAL or FEROCIOUS

Feral means 'wild', 'not (or no longer) domesticated'. It can be applied to people and occasionally to someone's appearance (a feral child is one who has been 'brought up' by animals). But the usual context is animal life—cats, pigeons and so on:
- ✓ One student, Anita, told of her holiday fun: she goes hunting for feral pigs with her nine dogs.

Though the adjective **ferocious** can mean 'cruel', it is more often found in the sense of 'intense':
- ✓ The company founder has also launched a ferocious campaign against its competitor.

FEWER or LESS

These words are frequently swapped for each other in speech and writing but formal English makes a distinction between them.

Both of these adjectival comparatives (few/fewer; little/less) indicate a smaller number or quantity. **Fewer** should be used when referring to a number of objects or people (i.e. with a plural noun):
- ✓ There were fewer swimmers in the pool today.

Less should be applied to any singular item or unit:
- ✓ Diet experts advise us to put less salt in our food.

FIANCE or FIANCEE

Both words are now slightly formal terms for people who are engaged to be married and the ending is an indication of gender.

A **fiancé** is the 'husband-to-be'; a **fiancée** is the 'wife-to-be'. (Each word takes an accent over the first 'e'.)

FLAIR or FLARE

Flair is a noun indicating a 'natural ability' in something (a flair for languages), while **flare** as a verb means to 'blaze out' or, as a noun, denotes a 'sudden light' (generally some kind of warning signal). It's this second spelling—**flares** describes the trousers of the 1970s. If the two words are confused it's usually because the second is used in error when the first is meant:

- ✓ He had a particular flare [should be flair] for recruiting new members.

FLAMMABLE, INFLAMMABLE or INFLAMMATORY

Ideas of 'going up in flames' underlie all three words but they have different uses. The first two words are interchangeable since the 'in-' prefix on the second does not turn it into a negative. The last term cannot be used in place of the other two.

The first two adjectives mean the same thing, 'capable of being (easily) set on fire'. The story goes that **flammable** was 'invented' because the 'in-' prefix on inflammable gave it the appearance of a negative (along the lines of 'visible/invisible'), thus suggesting that the object described could not be set on fire.

Inflammatory should not be applied to the fire-raising properties of a substance but rather means 'rousing strong feelings'. It normally describe comments or articles that, intentionally or otherwise, spark a protest.

FLAUNT or FLOUT

To **flaunt** is to 'make a public exhibition of', to 'show off'.

To **flout** is to 'treat something with contempt'; it's generally used when laws, rules, conventions are being disregarded—in a very public way:

✓ They flouted the law just to get publicity.

FLOTSAM or JETSAM

Flotsam describes 'any item lost during a shipwreck and later found floating in the water'. **Jetsam** applies to 'items which are deliberately thrown overboard' (e.g. to lighten the ship).

FLOUNDER or FOUNDER

These two verbs, very similar in sound and with associated meanings, are often misused.

To **flounder** is to 'struggle', to 'stumble':

✓ Without his cue card he was floundering for something to say.

To founder means to 'fall in ruins', to 'sink', and might be seen as the next (and last) stage after floundering. The verb is sometimes applied to horses, who might founder on the home straight, but most often to ships and, in a figurative sense, to people's schemes.

FLU or FLUE

Flu is the familiar and shortened form of 'influenza' (from an Italian word for 'influence' and following the old idea that diseases were the result of the malign effect of the 'stars').

The two words are occasionally confused, with the result that people appear to suffer from a chimney disease:

✓ Withdrawal symptoms included nausea, flue- [should be flu-] like symptoms, anxiety and sweating.

FOOLISH or FOOLHARDY

Both deriving from 'fool', these words carry distinct shades of meaning.

Foolish is applied to anybody or anything which the speaker or writer considers 'unwise or stupid'.

Foolhardy also means 'unwise' but with an overtone of 'impetuous' (i.e. foolish + hardy). There's sometimes a touch of admiration in the word when it carries the sense of 'risk-taking'.

FORBEAR or FOREBEAR

To forbear (with the stress falling on the second syllable) is to 'abstain', to 'hold back from'. The word is really for formal use, especially in its past tense form of forbore:
- ✓ He was severely criticised in the report but forbore from making a public response.

A **forebear** (which can also be spelled forbear but with the stress falling on the first syllable, regardless of spelling) is an 'ancestor', usually from several generations back.

FORBIDDING or FOREBODING

These words are different but they are both connected with the idea of threat, which is probably what causes any confusion.

Forbidding is an adjective with the sense of 'sinister', 'threatening' (usually in the appearance of people, buildings or places).

Foreboding is a noun which describes a 'feeling of unease'.

FORCEFUL, FORCIBLE or FORCED

Forceful, meaning 'with force' or 'vigorous', tends to be used about a person's character, attitude or words:
- ✓ He was a man of forceful personality and strong opinions.

Forcible can also be found in this sense of 'imposing' (a forceful/forcible speaker), but it more usually has a physical context and means 'employing force'—one step away from 'violent':
- ✓ The police made a forcible removal of the demonstrators from the scene.

Forced has a variety of meanings from 'strained' (a forced smile) to 'rapidly ripened' (forced fruit) and 'compelled' (forced removal).

FOREGO or FORGO

To **forego** is to 'go in front of'. It is hardly ever—or never—used except in the forms of foregoing and foregone (the foregoing points in an argument, a foregone conclusion).

To **forgo**, which has the alternative spelling forego, is to 'do without something':

- ✓ When his parents were away, he was obliged to forego his usual home food.

FOR EVER or FOREVER

As with 'every day/everyday' and 'every one/everyone', there is a slight and useful distinction between these two forms.

The one-word spelling can be used all the time—forever, one might say. But when 'eternally' is meant then the two-word for ever is preferred:

- ✓ The universe won't last for ever, you know.

In the sense of 'continually', 'all the time', the one-word form should be used:

- ✓ It's forever raining round these parts.

FORMALLY or FORMERLY

Formally means 'in the proper style', 'officially':

- ✓ The recent Congress meeting formally adopted laws protecting right to employment.

Formerly means 'at an earlier time':

- ✓ The money set aside for good causes is now being spent on projects that would formerly have been paid for out of general expenses.

FORTH or FOURTH

Forth is an old word meaning 'forward' or 'outward'. It appears as a prefix in words such as forthcoming or forthright, but is not used by itself now except in the phrase 'and so forth' or in the Bible 'Go forth and multiply'. This spelling is sometimes used by mistake for **fourth**, referring to the number 4.

FORTUITOUS or FORTUNATE

Fortuitous has gradually been encroaching on the territory of **fortunate**, and it is frequently used in the sense of the second word although its primary meaning is different.

Strictly speaking, **fortuitous** means occurring by chance:
- ✓ They were just talking about him when he made a fortuitous appearance at the meeting.

Fortunate is 'lucky':
- ✓ He was fortunate to receive only mild punishment for her mistakes.

But the similarity between the two words means that fortuitous is generally used to suggest an element of (good) luck combined with chance.

FULSOME or HEARTFELT

Fulsome is a tricky word to interpret because it often occurs in an ambiguous context. Meaning 'sickeningly admiring', it suggests hypocrisy.

But when **fulsome** is applied to, say, 'praise' or 'apology', it's not always clear whether the writer intends it in the (mistaken) sense of abundant, probably suggested by the 'ful-' prefix. If you want to convey sincerity then **heartfelt** is a better word, as it means what it says, i.e. 'deeply felt'.

GALLING or GRUELLING

Something which is **galling** is 'irritating'.

Gruelling means 'punishing', 'very tiring', and is applied to an experience or course which entails great physical or psychological stress.

GAMBIT, GAMUT or GAUNTLET

A **gambit** is an 'opening move', originally in chess (where the term applied to the deliberate sacrifice of a piece to gain an advantage).
Now the term is extended to any 'thought-out manoeuvre which begins a game, negotiation, etc.' A **gauntlet** refers to a glove.

GAMBLE or GAMBOL

To **gamble** is to 'risk' or to 'play for money':
- ✓ Some come to gamble high stakes.

To **gambol** is to 'leap around playfully':
- ✓ Our pets need to be allowed to frolic and gambol.

(The past tense forms of each word are gambled and gambolled.)

GARNER or GARNISH

These similar-sounding words are occasionally confused, perhaps through some indirect link between ideas of food and harvest.
Connected to granary (a storehouse for grain), **garner** means to 'gather up':
- ✓ He has garnered particular critical acclaim for his novels.

To **garnish** is to 'decorate'. The word, which is verb or noun, is most often found in recipes, descriptions of dishes, etc. and refers to the small additions intended to make a meal look good and taste better.

GEEZER or GEYSER

Identical pronunciation sometimes causes confusion here.
Geezer is a slang term for a 'man' (previously an old one).
A **geyser** is a 'hot spring, of water, mud or steam':
- ✓ The volcano has been restless since 2001, with increased numbers of earthquakes, rising lake temperatures and geysers of boiling mud.

GOURMAND or GOURMET

There is widespread uncertainty over the distinction between a gourmand and a gourmet.

Being called a **gourmand** is not a compliment since it means a 'glutton', a greedy eater who doesn't mind what goes down as long as he/she gets enough of it.

A **gourmet** is a 'person with refined tastes in food and drink'. The word is also an adjective meaning 'refined', as here:

✓ The Chef wants to produce a gourmet meal in 30 minutes flat.

GRAND or GRANDIOSE

These two look alike but more separates them than unites them.

The difference between the adjectives is that **grand** should be applied to something which is authentically 'splendid', while **grandiose** suggests that what is described is somehow 'inflated' or 'false'.

A **grand** building is large and very imposing; a grand scheme is ambitious and conceived on a great scale. **Grandiose** ideas, by contrast, are hollow; they sound good but will never amount to anything.

GRILL or GRILLE

Both words describe metallic, perforated frames, and the frequent appearance of **grilled** (as in grilled meat) encourages the error of using the second where the first is intended.

A **grill** is a 'metal frame used in cooking':

✓ She likes to cook on the gas grill.

A **grille** is a 'metal screen in front of a window or car radiator'.

GRISLY or GRIZZLY

Grisly is an adjective meaning 'terrible', 'gruesome'.

Grizzly means 'of a grey colour' (the same as 'grizzled'). In its noun use it stands for the grizzly bear (whose scientific name is Ursus), usually just referred to as the 'grizzly'.

HANGED or HUNG

These are the past tense forms of the verb to hang. There's a tendency to use hung for everything and everybody. Hanged should be used in one context, however.

In general things should be **hung**. Pictures on walls, coats on racks, meat in the butcher's; **hung** can apply even to people when they are clinging on to something:

✓ He hung from the window sill by his fingertips.

The single exception is in the context of capital punishment, when the individual is hanged. The wrong form of the word is often used:

✓ He was arrested immediately, found guilty of 'moral insanity' and hung [should be hanged].

HEROIN or HEROINE

That final 'e' makes all the difference, and the slip is easily made.

Heroin is the 'drug which is a morphine derivative', while **heroine** is the female equivalent of 'hero', a 'woman who shows heroic qualities' or the 'central woman character either in real life or in a story, film, etc.'

HISTORIC or HISTORICAL

Both of these terms derive from history but they carry fairly distinct meanings.

Historical is an adjective meaning 'relating to history', and attaching it to a noun says nothing about the significance of that noun. It's a 'neutral' word. **Historic** means significant.

✓ It was a historic moment in the history of India.

HOARD or HORDE

These two have the same sound and share overlapping ideas of mass and quantity.

A **hoard** is a 'hidden store' of something, usually valuable and put by for use in the future.

Horde describes a 'large number':

✓ There were hordes of people in the market for the sales.

HUMILIATION or HUMILITY

Humiliation is 'shame' or 'treatment which hurts a person's self-respect'. The humiliation may be intended or unintended.

Humility is 'modesty', the 'capacity of being humble'.

I

ILLEGIBLE or UNREADABLE

These two words both convey the idea of 'hard to read' but they have two different senses which are reflected in their definitions.

Illegible refers to the physical appearance of handwriting or print and means 'hard or impossible to read'. **Unreadable** can be used in this sense too although its principal application is to the quality of someone's writing, where it means 'so poor as to be not worth reading'.

IMPLY or INFER

To **imply** something is to 'hint' or 'suggest' it without its being openly stated.

To **infer** is to 'draw conclusions from the evidence', and suggests skill at understanding hints and working out implications.

Infer is sometimes used as though it meant imply — as in the erroneous 'I don't like your tone of voice. What are you inferring?' This usage is wrong by the standards of correct English.

INDIGNITY or INDIGNATION

An **indignity** is something that is inflicted or endured, an 'insult' or 'humiliation.'

Indignation is what the sufferer may feel about it afterwards, a sense of 'justified anger'. Indignation can be expressed on behalf of others and the unfair treatment they have received, as well as being felt for one's own sake.

INDUSTRIAL or INDUSTRIOUS

Both of these adjectives derive from 'industry' but they have acquired distinct meanings.

Industrial is used of objects, places, processes, etc. and means 'connected with industry or the manufacture of goods':
- ✓ Industrial output remained high in the second quarter of the year.

Industrious is used only of individuals or groups of people and means 'diligent', 'hard-working'.

INFORMANT or INFORMER

Although both of these nouns describe a 'person who passes over information', they are used in different circumstances, one of which is more positive than the other.

An **informant** is a 'source' (who may be acting out of a sense of public duty to blow the whistle on wrongdoing, for example) and the stress is on the data he/she passes over.

The term **informer**, also describing a 'source', tends to be restricted to the person who names names, especially in police contexts.

INGENIOUS or INGENUOUS

Two words with a single-letter difference: They look as though they should be related but they are near-opposites.

Ingenious means 'clever', particularly in the context of finding solutions for problems or thinking up new methods.

Ingenuous means 'artless', 'simple' — usually too much so, as it's not innocence so much as gullibility that is suggested:

- ✓ When he spoke about money it was with an ingenuous enthusiasm that offended no one.

INHUMAN or INHUMANE

Both adjectives convey strong condemnation, and many people use them interchangeably. However, there is a distinction.

Inhuman, meaning 'brutal', 'barbarous', is the harsher of the two, and can describe an individual without any redeeming (human) features. More generally, it characterizes people's behaviour towards each other, with the implication of being less than, not worthy of, a human being:

- ✓ We recall the inhuman treatment of concentration camp inmates.

Inhumane has the sense of 'cruel', 'lacking in qualities of kindness and sympathy', and is the opposite of 'humane'. It can be used about the way individuals or animals are treated.

INNOVATION or INVENTION

These two are closely connected but in no way mean the same thing.

An **innovation** is the 'introduction of something fresh' — not as radical as an invention, it's usually the development or refinement of an existing idea or system.

By contrast, an **invention** is a 'new device or discovery':

- ✓ Marconi is generally credited with the invention of wireless telegraphy.

Invention is also used in the sense of fiction — a 'deceit or lie'.

INNUENDO or INSINUATION

Both words describe something not openly stated but implied.

An **innuendo** is an 'indirect remark', very frequently one with sexual overtones—it's often the equivalent of the French phrase 'double entendre'.

An **insinuation** is more general, being any 'hint carrying an unpleasant suggestion'.

(To insinuate is to 'hint' but also to 'work (oneself) gradually into a place'—an organization, a person's good books—by stealth.)

INOCULATE or VACCINATE

Two 'medical' terms that may appear to have distinct meanings but can, in fact, be used interchangeably in most contexts.

To **inoculate** is to 'protect against disease' by infecting someone with a mild form of that disease, so ensuring future immunity.

To **vaccinate** was originally to 'protect against smallpox by using the cowpox virus' (vacca is Latin for 'cow'). The word is now interchangeable with inoculate and applies to providing comparable protection from any disease.

INSIDIOUS or INVIDIOUS

Insidious points to a kind of slow-burning malice, and means 'cunning'. It can be applied to people but is more often used to describe words, attitudes, effects.

Invidious means 'causing bad feeling' or 'provoking envy'. Often qualifying 'position' or 'distinction', it should not be used as a synonym for 'difficult'.

INTENSE or INTENSIVE

Intense means 'strong' or 'characterized by extreme emotion'.

While **intense** can be used about people, **intensive**—meaning 'thorough', 'without relief or let-up'—characterizes things like research and investigation.

INTERMENT or INTERNMENT

Interment is 'burial', almost always used literally.

Internment is 'confinement' (in a prison or camp). The word usually describes the pre-emptive treatment meted out to those regarded as potential troublemakers, spies, terrorists, etc.—that is, they are locked up as a 'precaution' and without the benefit of trial.

(The associated verbs are inter and intern. **Intern** is also a noun meaning a 'trainee doctor in a hospital' or a 'person getting experience in any profession'.)

INVEIGH or INVEIGLE

These are two slightly unusual words which are sometimes confused, perhaps because of their similar spellings.

To **inveigh** (pronounced to rhyme with 'say' and always followed by 'against') is to 'attack strongly', usually in speech.

To **inveigle** (pronounced to rhyme with 'bagel') is to 'tempt' or 'coax'. The word carries the hint of something underhand.

ITS or IT'S

This is one of the commonest and most basic mistakes in written English. It's the apostrophe which causes the problem, of course.

It's is the contracted or shortened form of it is or it has:
- ✓ It's a warm day.
- ✓ It's been raining all day.

Its, without an apostrophe, is the possessive form of the pronoun it:
- ✓ The cat flicked its tail.

JUNCTION or JUNCTURE

Both words mean a 'joining or union' but occur in different contexts.

Junction tends to have a physical application, describing the point where roads or railway lines or electric wires meet. **Juncture** is a coming together in time rather than space, and suggests a 'critical point' in some process:
- ✓ At that juncture Dharmender and Hema Malini were able to announce their love to each other—but not to the world.

K

KNELL or KNOLL

A **knell** describes the 'sound of a tolling bell'—particularly at a funeral. In fact the word is almost always used figuratively and prefaced with 'death'.

The verb is also knell (past tense knelled).

A **knoll** is a 'small hill'.

L

LAMA or LLAMA

It is surely the exotic source of these words—one from Tibetan, the other from Spanish via a Peruvian language—that sometimes causes confusion. There is nothing in them to hint at the meaning and so guide the spelling.

The **lama** with one 'l' is a 'Buddhist monk in Tibet'.

The **llama** with two 'l's is a 'four-legged beast of burden', the South American equivalent of the camel (in fact camels and llamas are related).

LARVA or LAVA

A **larva** (plural larvae) is an 'animal, usually an insect, in the earliest stages of its development'.

Lava is 'molten rock from a volcano'.

LAST or LATTER

Last applies to anything coming at the end of a sequence (the last word, her last book) and means 'final', 'most recent'. **Latter,** whom properly used, should apply to the 'second of two items'.

LATITUDE or LONGITUDE

Latitude is the 'angular distance from the equator, measured to the north or south'. Latitude has the additional meanings of 'range' or 'freedom'. **Longitude** uses the meridian, any one of the great and imaginary circles running from pole to pole, with the meridian line through Greenwich taken as the starting point. Longitude is therefore the 'angular distance between a particular place and the Greenwich meridian, measured to the east and west'.

LAY or LIE

To **lay** is to 'put down' and is a transitive verb (i.e. one which is generally followed by an object):
- ✓ Lay your sleeping head, my love… (first line of poem by W. H. Auden)

To **lie** is to 'be at rest on a horizontal surface' and is an intransitive verb (one which is not followed by a direct object):
- ✓ He told the dog to lie down at once.

Confusion mostly arises from the fact that the past tense of lie is lay:
- ✓ The dog lay down and went to sleep straightaway.

The past tense of lie is laid:
- ✓ They laid the picnic food out on the mat.

The past participle form (i.e. the one used after 'has' or 'had') is lain for lie:
- ✓ The farmhouse has lain empty for almost two years now.

LEACH or LEECH

To **leach** (only a verb) is to 'filter in or out'.

To **leech** is to 'suck the blood out of', to 'drain', from the noun leech, a 'blood-sucking worm'. Leech is frequently used to describe any parasitic individual or organization.

LESSEE or LESSOR

This pair of 'legalistic' terms is quite easy to confuse.

The **lessee** is the 'person to whom a lease is granted' (usually in property) while a **lessor** is the 'person who grants the lease'. A 'leaseholder' is the same as a lessee and a 'letter' (i.e. a person who lets) is the equivalent of lessor.

LIBEL or SLANDER

Both nouns and verbs, **libel** and **slander** refer to a 'defamatory accusation' or mean to 'defame'. **Libel** is used about anything written or presented in permanent form, including material on the Internet.

Slander tends to be reserved for spoken comments.

LIBERTARIAN or LIBERTINE

These two words derive from 'liberty' so it's perhaps appropriate that they have moved off in different directions. One describes a political or ideological position while the other characterizes a person who pursues sexual pleasure.

A **libertarian** is a 'person who believes in the maximum possible amount of freedom for himself/herself and others'. This usually entails freedom under the law but includes the right to pursue behaviour that might be self-destructive. The word is often associated with a particular branch of right-wing thinking.

A **libertine** is a 'person who leads a dissolute life, especially in sexual matters'.

LICENCE or LICENSE

This is a distinction that only emerges when the words are written.
The noun form is **licence**—TV licence; driver's licence; off-licence—while the verb is **license**:

✓ 'Are you licensed to drive this vehicle, sir?'

LIGHTNING or LIGHTENING

Lightning, as an adjective, applies to anything which is 'moving very

fast', and as a noun is the accompaniment of thunder, a 'burst of light in the sky':
- ✓ He was struck by lightning on the set.

This spelling is sometimes confused with **lightening,** meaning 'making lighter' (applied to reducing a burden or to changing a colour).

LIMP, LIMPID or LUCID

Limpid looks as though it must be connected to limp. It isn't. Its proper association is with lucid.

Limp means 'drooping', 'lacking firmness and authority'.

Limpid has nothing to do with the previous word but, if anything, is a near-opposite since it means 'very clear', 'transparent'. Frequently applied to music performances — often those at the piano, for some reason — it can also be used in more literal contexts.

Lucid has the same sense of 'very clear' and therefore 'easy to understand'. The context here is normally language, books, explanations.

LIVID or LURID

Both of these similar-sounding adjectives have connections with colour but are most widely used in other contexts.

Livid is 'dark', 'leaden':
- ✓ His cheeks are livid with bruises.

But it's most frequently used to mean 'extremely angry' (presumably because of the colour of an angry face).

Lurid has been used about a range of colour tones, from pale yellow to purple. In another sense it is also a favourite tabloid expression, generally applied now to news stories which have a 'sensational' quality.

LOATH or LOATHE

Loath — with or, occasionally, without the middle a — is an adjective indicating reluctance, being 'unwilling':

✓ I'd be loath to get involved in their quarrels.

Loathe is a verb meaning to 'regard with disgust':

✓ She loathed his mannerism.

LOSE, LOOSE or LOOSEN

In their verb forms these words are occasionally confused, particularly the first two because of the doubling of the 'o'. To **lose** or 'mislay' has one:

✓ The crowd on the streets in the old part of town made it easy to lose one's way.

To **loose** is to 'set free', 'cast off'.

To **loosen** is to 'make looser', to 'untighten', either literally or figuratively:

✓ Too many drinks certainly loosened his tongue.

(The past tense forms are lost, loosed and loosened, respectively.)

LUSTFUL or LUSTY

Although both of these adjectives derive from lust, the meaning of one is essentially innocent.

Lustful is only connected to sex. It means full of 'lust', 'sensual', and hints at something passionate and perhaps forbidden:

✓ Boredom at work could be manifested by lustful dreams about a colleague.

Even when **lusty** enters the sexual stakes the word has a jauntiness to it which is lacking in the altogether more biblical-sounding lustful.

LUXURIANT or LUXURIOUS

Both adjectives derive from luxury but have distinct meanings which shouldn't be confused.

Luxuriant describes anything which is 'produced in abundant quantities' or is 'lush'—its use is generally restricted to natural growth (hair, foliage, etc.).

Luxurious conveys notions 'of great comfort', expense and (sometimes) flashiness.

M

MACHO, MANLY or MANNISH

All of these terms relate to masculinity but they apply in quite different contexts.
Manly means 'brave', 'fitting for a man'.
Macho — from the Spanish word for 'male' — is a rough contemporary version but carries a suggestion of swaggering masculinity.
Mannish can be applied to women who are considered insufficiently feminine.

MAJORITY or MOST OF

Majority is a noun meaning 'the greater number':
- ✓ The majority of the people in the poll favoured the right wing.

Majority should not be used to mean 'the larger part' of something which cannot be split up into individual elements. When referring to a single unit, most of should be used, or another expression such as 'the greater part of':
- ✓ I was on tenterhooks for the **most of** the film.

MALEVOLENT, MALICIOUS or MALIGNANT

Malevolent and **malicious** apply to individuals and their words or actions, in the sense of 'ill-disposed', 'wishing harm to'.
Malevolent is also used of animals. **Malicious** is perhaps less strong; a malicious remark (i.e. one that shows malice) may be nothing more than 'spiteful' while a malevolent one suggests something darker and more deep-rooted.
Malignant contains these meanings but, as indicated by its frequent application to cancerous tumours; it carries the more intense sense of 'causing harm or evil to'.

MANTEL or MANTLE

A **mantel** (usually mantelpiece) is the 'shelf above a fireplace'.

A **mantle** is a 'cloak or covering', but the word is very often applied metaphorically to mean 'status', 'authority'. In particular the handing over of a mantle suggests the symbolic moment when power changes hands.

MASTERFUL or MASTERLY

These two terms deriving from 'master' have an overlap of meaning but can carry different emphases.

The adjective **masterly** means 'highly skilled', 'brilliantly accomplished', and is most often used when a performance is being praised.

Masterful is often used to mean the same thing, but it carries overtones of 'bullying', of aggressive assertion, even if this is intended in a complimentary way.

MAY or MIGHT

There is a growing tendency to use **may** in all circumstances, even where might would be correct.

May is the present tense form:
- ✓ We think he may go. (But we don't know yet whether he's going to.)

Might is the past tense:
- ✓ We thought he might go. (Either he did go or he didn't, but the sentence implies that we know one way or the other.)

MAY BE or MAYBE

As with other pairs such as 'all ready/already', the two-word version of may be is hardly distinguished in pronunciation from the single word. But when a mistake is made in writing the wrong meaning results.

May be is a combination of two verbs and is used when talking about a possibility:
- ✓ He hasn't answered but it may be that he didn't get my letter.

Maybe (one word) means 'perhaps':
- ✓ He hasn't answered but maybe he didn't get my letter.

MEDIA or MEDIUM

Media, a collective term for 'means of communication such as television or newspapers', is the plural form of **medium**. As a plural it should take the appropriate verb form:
- ✓ The media are influential in shaping people's opinions. The tendency is to treat the word as a singular noun (an 'it' rather than a 'they').

MEDICAL or MEDICINAL

Both of these words are obviously connected to health and sickness but they have slightly different applications.

Medical means 'relating to the practice of medicine' (medical student, medical insurance) and, as a noun, describes a 'physical examination to check a person's health/fitness'.

The adjective **medicinal** means 'used in medicine' and so 'helping to cure'.

MERETRICIOUS or MERITORIOUS

Meretricious derives from the Latin word **meretrix** meaning 'prostitute', and indeed its primary sense is 'relating to prostitution'. Never used in this sense now, it has come to mean 'flashy but without substance'.

Meritorious means 'worth praising':
- ✓ Being healthy is not meritorious in itself.

METAL or METTLE

Metal describes 'any of the elementary substances such as gold or iron'. This spelling is sometimes used when mettle is meant. The confusion isn't surprising since both words are pronounced the same, and **mettle** carries the metallic-sounding idea of 'hardness', 'spirit'. When people are 'on their mettle' they are put in a situation in which they have to prove themselves.

METEOR or METEORITE

These two words refer to the same object but in a 'before and after' sense.

A **meteor** is a 'small object which turns to a fireball when it enters the earth's atmosphere'. Even small ones can do damage and the impact of anything larger could be terminal.

The term meteor can also apply to 'anything or anybody whose progress is bright but brief'.

More usual is the adjective **meteoric** to describe such a progress, often coupled with 'rise', as in 'her meteoric rise to the top of his profession'. **Meteors** do the reverse of going up, of course, although a belief stretching back as far as the ancient Greeks held that comets and other such objects actually emanated from the earth.)

A **meteorite** is what the meteor becomes when it has hit the earth—a 'lump of stone or metal':

✓ A meteorite from the Red Planet had been located in Antarctica.

METER or METRE

A **meter** is a 'measuring instrument': parking meter; thermometer; milometer.

A **metre** is the 'basic unit of length in the metric system'(three metres in length, a kilometre further on). This is the spelling that is also used to describe poetic 'rhythm', the contrasting sounds between long and short or stressed and unstressed syllables in verse.

METHOD or METHODOLOGY

The longer, more impressive-sounding word is sometimes preferred to the shorter, more familiar one.

A **method** is a 'procedure' and a **methodology** is a 'system of procedures'. Methodology is a popular word in certain writing.

MILITATE or MITIGATE

To **militate,** generally followed by 'against', is to 'have weight', to 'operate'.

Mitigate has something of an opposite meaning—it is to 'lighten', to 'make less harsh'.

MISANTHROPIST or MISOGYNIST

Both of these terms are to do with dislike and hatred but one has a restricted sexual sense.

Misanthropy is a 'generalised distrust or hatred of everybody', men, women and children.

Misogyny is specifically 'hatred of women'.

MOMENTARY or MOMENTOUS

Both words derive from different senses of the same word, moment, but they can convey almost opposite meanings.

Anything which is **momentary** (pronounced with the stress on the first syllable) is very 'short-lived'.

Momentous (pronounced with the stress on the second syllable) means 'highly significant'.

MORAL or MORALE

Moral as an adjective means 'connected to questions of right and wrong':

✓ 'We are not going to be moral guardians and stand in judgement.'

As a noun, moral is used in the singular only in the sense of 'lesson' (the moral of a story). In the plural, morals describes the 'principles or guiding beliefs' of a person or group, although it tends to have a sexual application only.

Morale characterizes the 'spirit of an organized group' such as a body of soldiers or a cricket team.
- ✓ Their morale was sapped when many soldiers were killed.

MUCOUS or MUCUS

One of these words is a noun while the other is the adjective derived from it, and it is easy to confuse the two spellings.

Mucus is the noun, describing the fluid secreted by a bodily membrane (e.g. the nose) in humans or animals.

Mucous is the adjective meaning 'mucus-like or slimy':
- ✓ Direct contact with sulphuric acid will burn the skin and play havoc with mucous membranes.

MUNDANE or WORLDLY

Both terms mean 'of this world', but mundane carries the sense of 'everyday' (to the point of being boring).

Worldly is often used as part of compound words ('worldly-wise', 'other-worldly') but it also has a meaning of 'experienced in the ways of the world', 'sophisticated'.

N

NAKED or NUDE

This is quite a difficult distinction—and naturally an interesting one.

Naked is the more versatile word with its senses of 'without assistance' or 'lacking ornament' (naked effort, naked truth) as well as the basic meanings of 'bare', 'uncovered'. Naked is generally a less loaded or emotive word than **nude**.

Nude has associations with painting, photography and porn, and to that extent it could be equated with being 'intentionally naked'—often for artistic or sexual purposes.

The words aren't quite interchangeable.

NAVAL or NAVEL

The adjective **naval** means 'relating to the navy'. The noun **navel** is defined by one dictionary as the 'depression in the centre of the abdomen' but is known to the rest of humanity as the 'belly/tummy-button'.

NEGLECTFUL, NEGLIGENT or NEGLIGIBLE

Neglectful means 'inattentive', with the implication of failing to care for something or somebody:
- ✓ His busy life at work made him a rather neglectful father.

Negligent means 'careless', particularly in relation to matters which are your responsibility and for which you may be held accountable.

Negligible means 'very slight or unimportant' (and therefore able to be neglected).

NICENESS or NICETY

Niceness means the 'quality of being nice', 'agreeableness'. There's a blandness to the word or to what it describes, and it's often used with just a touch of criticism.

Nicety means 'precision' (as when something is judged to a nicety) or 'refinement' when it is usually found in the plural form, niceties.

O

OBJECTIVE or SUBJECTIVE

An **objective** approach is one which is 'unaffected by personal feelings', 'detached'.

Subjective means 'personal', 'taking one's feelings into account':
- ✓ From a subjective view point she judged him.

OBSOLESCENT or OBSOLETE

Obsolescent means 'going out of date'.
Something which is **obsolete** is 'old', 'out of date' (and so useless).

OFFICIAL or OFFICIOUS

Both of these terms originally derive from the same Latin source but they have very different meanings. The second is sometimes used by mistake for the first, perhaps because people occasionally find that officials can also be officious.

As an adjective **official** describes a 'person or process that is properly authorised'.

The noun official is used of someone employed by a government department, as 'senior PMO officials'.

The adjective **officious,** by contrast, means 'interfering'.

- ✓ 'What are you two talking about?' he asked in his usual officious manner.

ORDINANCE or ORDNANCE

The one-letter difference between these two words, and the fact that pronunciation hardly distinguishes between them, can cause problems.

Ordinance has the sense of a 'ruling' or 'decree' (especially in a local context):

- ✓ In India an ordinance can be made by the parliament.

Ordnance has the general sense of 'military equipment' but is almost always restricted in its application to 'artillery and ammunition'.

OUTSIDE or OUTSIDE OF

There's not much justification for writing outside of when a simple outside would do. This is specially the case when **outside** refers to a place:

- ✓ They used to meet outside the building. (not outside of)

When referring to time, **outside** of is quite often used:
- ✓ They used to meet outside of office hours. (but outside would do just as well)

But when 'apart from' is meant, outside of is more acceptable:
- ✓ He had few interests outside of his work.

P

PANDA or PANDER

One of these words is a cuddly-looking animal, the other is a pimp. Take care over spelling.

The **panda** is the 'bear-like animal' from China (as well as a rather less well-known raccoon-like Himalayan creature).

It's not to be confused with a **pander** (sometimes spelled pandar) who is a 'pimp' or 'go-between'—the word has a slightly literary flavour but is always derogatory. As a verb, to pander is to 'gratify', to 'cater to the (low) taste of others':
- ✓ Maybe when they started price-cutting they felt they had to pander to the working class.

PEDAL or PEDDLE

Pedal as a noun describes a 'lever worked by the foot'; as a verb it is to 'operate such a lever':
- ✓ I pedalled fast to keep pace with the other bikes.

Pedaller is the associated noun. **Peddle**, a verb, is to 'sell small items'. When applied to any other kind of trade there is the suggestion of sleaziness or illegality: peddling drugs. Even when it's used in ordinary contexts it tends to disparage what is being 'sold'.

PEOPLE, PEOPLES or PERSONS

People means either an '(unspecified) number of individuals' or a 'whole national/racial/ethnic group' (the German people, the Indian people).

The plural **peoples** is restricted to this second sense and applies to the 'nations/racial groups of the world'—it's a slightly formal expression. The plural **persons** is formal and bureaucratic, and the only appropriate place for it is on notices ('This bus seats 54 persons').

PERPETRATE or PERPETUATE

These quite similar-sounding words both contain the idea of 'carrying on/out'.

To **perpetrate** is to 'carry out', to 'commit'. The noun that accompanies the verb is often 'crime' or 'outrage'.

To **perpetuate** is to 'sustain', to 'make last':
- ✓ The story writer never perpetuates the traditional literary myths of romantic love and happy endings.

PERQUISITE or PREREQUISITE

Both terms describe something which is conditional or dependent.

A **perquisite** is a 'benefit arising from employment'. The word is usually shortened to perk—as in 'perks of the job'—and would only be spelled out in full in fairly formal contexts:
- ✓ Among the perquisites of this position are frequent foreign travel and a generous entertainment allowance.

A **prerequisite** is a 'condition that must be met beforehand':
- ✓ A NET certification is the prerequisite to become a college teacher.

PERSECUTE or PROSECUTE

To **persecute** is to 'maintain a campaign of harassment' (particularly for political or religious reasons).
- ✓ First-time offenders may be warned by the police rather than prosecuted.

(Prosecute has the less familiar meaning of to 'pursue in order to accomplish'; in this sense a war or a political campaign can be prosecuted.)

PERSON or PERSONA

The Latin word for 'person' is persona in expressions such as 'persona non grata'. But in English a person and his/her persona are not at all the same thing.

A **person** is just a person, a 'human being' (and the word often carries a slightly dismissive note).

But a **persona** (plural personae) is something else—a 'public image', the 'face' assumed when dealing with the outside world'.

PERSONAL or PERSONNEL

Personal is an adjective only, meaning 'relating to the individual', although it very often carries the additional meaning of 'private':
- ✓ He was unwilling to reveal his personal reasons for rejecting the job.

Personnel is a collective noun which describes the 'workforce' in a particular organization. It's a bureaucratic word—rather impersonal in fact.

PERSPECTIVE, PROSPECTIVE or PROSPECTUS

This similar-sounding group contains ideas of views and visions.

A **perspective** is a 'point of view'. It's probably most widely used in the phrase 'put into perspective', which derives from the artistic technique of showing on a two-dimensional surface how objects seem smaller in the distance. So perspective becomes a way of assessing the relative importance—or lack of importance—of something, usually a problem.

The adjective **prospective** refers to the future and means 'expected', 'probable'.

A **prospectus** is the 'outline of some project which will materialize in the future' or it describes the advertising brochure issued by schools, colleges, etc.

PERVERSE or PERVERTED

Perverse describes a person or an action that is 'contrary', obstinate', something hard to account for rationally.

Perverted has a sexual application almost exclusively, and characterises behaviour or attitudes that are 'deviant'.

As a verb pervert (stress on second syllable) is most frequently found in a legal context: to pervert the course of justice is to 'interfere with the proper process of the law' (by threats, bribes, etc.).

PHENOMENON or PHENOMENAL

A **phenomenon** is no more than an 'observable event':
- ✓ Bluffing about books is a universal phenomenon.

The adjective **phenomenal** is almost always used in this sense and signifies anything 'outstanding'.

PIQUE or PIQUANCY

These related terms, both derived from French, characterize emotions or sensations that are linked by the idea of 'sharpness'.

Pique is 'bad feeling', 'wounded pride'.

(Pique is also a verb with the same meaning: to 'wound' or 'irritate'.)

Piquancy, a noun meaning 'sharpness', is often used to describe taste, particularly in its adjectival form (a piquant sauce), and generally has positive overtones.

PITEOUS, PITIABLE, PITIFUL or PATHETIC

Pitiable and **pitiful** can be applied to people and situations. Of the two pitiful is perhaps slightly stronger, suggesting someone who arouses pity through some visible means as well as by inner suffering, while **pitiable** is more to do with the latter:
- ✓ The people heard the piteous sounds of the trapped cat.

Both adjectives are also used to indicate mockery (a pitiful attempt).

Pathetic has a milder meaning of 'arousing sympathy', but usually carries an overtone, if not of contempt, then of superiority.

The colloquial use of **pathetic** to mean 'useless', or, more casually, as a term passing judgement on an unsatisfactory situation, can sometimes be a source of ambiguity:
- ✓ He looks pathetic in a cotton suit.

POPULOUS, POPULAR or POPULIST

Populous indicates that an area is 'densely populated' (all cities are populous by definition), while **popular** means 'in favour', 'liked by many, or 'involving many people'.

Populist (noun and adjective) generally occurs in a political context and describes 'somebody who aims to appeal to the majority' (by offering sops).

PORE or POUR

The two verbs are sometimes confused, partly because they sound identical but also because both are frequently followed by 'over'.

To **pore** is to 'examine carefully'.

To **pour** is to 'make flow'.

PORT or STARBOARD

Port is the left-hand side on ships (and on aircraft) while the **starboard** side is to the right, when facing forward.

PORTENTOUS or PRETENTIOUS

There's some overlap between these two weighty words but also a distinction.

Portentous comes from portent and so means 'ominous' or 'full of significance'. But it usually has the sense of 'self-important' too, and is rarely meant in a complimentary sense.

Pretentious also means 'self-important' shading into 'pompous'.

PRACTICAL or PRACTICABLE

A **practical** person or idea is a 'sensible and realistic' one. When

applied to a plan, it suggests not only that it can be realized but also that it has merits:
- ✓ He soon came up with some practical ways of getting round the problem.

Practical carries the additional senses of 'good at making things' and 'down to earth' or 'actual' (as in practical experience as opposed to theoretical knowledge).

Practicable is not used about people, and indicates merely that something 'can be achieved', and not necessarily that it ought to be:
- ✓ Within the next few decades it is expected that manned flights to Mars will become practicable.

PRACTICE or PRACTISE

This is one of a group of word pairs which change by one letter between noun and verb (see also 'advice/advise', 'licence/license', etc.), and is probably the pair which is most often confused.

The **practice** spelled with a 'c' is the noun:
- ✓ There are parallels between Indian and British business practices.

While the practise with an **'s'** is the verb:
- ✓ The band practised for most of the day.

PRAY or PREY

To **pray** is to 'beg for' or to 'ask during worship'.

To **prey** (on) is to 'kill for food' or to 'exploit' (with the suggestion of terrorizing). (The victim is the prey while the attacker is the predator.)

PRECIPITATE or PRECIPITOUS

Precipitate, as an adjective, describes an action that is 'rushed', 'headlong'. As a verb it means to 'produce abruptly'.

Precipitous means 'steep':
- ✓ The steep mountain was extremely deep, and unusually precipitous.

PRESCRIBE or PROSCRIBE

A one-letter difference changes one word into its near opposite.
To **prescribe** is to 'direct', to 'lay down as a rule':
- ✓ The doctor prescribed plenty of rest and exercise.

To **proscribe** is to 'ban':
- ✓ The book has been proscribed by the Church.

PREVARICATE or PROCRASTINATE

To **prevaricate** is to 'avoid giving a straight answer'. Not as outright as lying, it is still evading the truth.
To **procrastinate** is to hesitate and delay:
- ✓ To be or not to be.

(The noun forms are **prevarication** and **procrastination**.)

PRINCIPAL or PRINCIPLE

Principal is both noun and adjective, and means 'most important':
- ✓ The principal thing to remember, she was told, was discipline.

The most frequent application of the noun is to describe the 'head of a college or a school'. An additional noun meaning of **principal** is 'money on which interest is paid'.

Principle is a noun only, and means 'basic belief':
- ✓ My father was a man of principles.

PRISE or PRIZE

To prise is to 'force (open or away from)', using something as a lever—e.g. a crowbar or money.

Prized could be used in the example above, but prised is more usual in British English.

A **prize** is a 'reward', and the verb means to 'place a high value on'.

PRODIGY or PROTEGE

A **prodigy** is a 'wonder'. Once used about signs and omens, it is now applied only to people. It's often associated with children who show very great talent in some field.

The word should not be confused with **protege** (more correctly spelled protégé), which describes a 'person who is under another's patronage or protection'.

PROGRAM or PROGRAMME

There is a tendency to use the increasingly familiar first spelling for all occasions in British English.

In the US, all **programs**, theatre, television, computer, are just that—programs.

British English has a spelling difference between the **programme** which you buy in the theatre, watch on TV etc., and the program which runs on a computer.

PROPHECY or PROPHESY

Prophecy, meaning 'prediction' and pronounced to rhyme with 'see', is a noun:
- ✓ The prophecy that the world was about to end is in the Book of Revelations.

To **prophesy,** to 'foretell', is a verb (pronounced to rhyme with 'sigh'). The verb doesn't carry quite the religious/messianic overtones of the noun, and can be used in the sense of 'forecast':
- ✓ The Aleph company prophesied continued growth for the rest of the year.

PSEUDONYM, PEN NAME or NOM DE PLUME

A **pseudonym** is a 'fictitious name', sometimes one assumed by writers but often by other people to ensure anonymity or protection.

A **nom de plume** is the same as a **pen name**; specifically a 'writer's assumed name' (as Mary Anne Evans took the name George Eliot at the beginning of her literary career). Oddly, nom de plume is not actually used in French—it joins a little list of phrases which you don't find in that country including 'son et lumière'.

Q

QUASH or SQUASH

In a legal context, to **quash** is to 'make invalid' (convictions can bequashed or overturned). It has the more general sense of to 'crush out of existence' but not in a literal sense.

Apart from noun senses like 'fruit' and 'ball game', **squash** as a verb has the same meaning of to 'crush flat'. There's a more 'physical' quality to squash, which can be used both metaphorically and literally.

R

REBOUND or REDOUND

To **rebound** is to 'spring back'. Even when not used literally, which it generally isn't, the word retains a kind of physical spring.

To **redound** is also to 'rebound' or 'be reflected back', but this rarer word is found in more dignified contexts: Balls don't redound, but words and behaviour do—to your or someone else's advantage, disadvantage, etc.:

✓ His policy always was to do what redounded to the credit of his wife.

RECOURSE, RESOURCE or RESORT

To have **recourse** to something means to go to it as a 'source of aid'.

Resort could be used as the verb. ('We resorted to…'). This is more usual than the equivalent noun construction ('We had resort to…').

A **resource** is also a 'source of help', but the word doesn't normally convey the idea of turning to something in an emergency or a difficulty. More often it carries the related sense of a 'means' that one can draw on (a means of financial support, a way of filling one's time, etc.):

✓ He led a comfortable life after retirement as he had plenty of resources.

Resource can also be a verb, usually in participle form: 'a properly resourced library'.

REGARDLESS or IRREGARDLESS

One of these words does not exist.

Regardless means 'without regard to', 'without taking into consideration'.

Irregardless does not—or at least should not—exist. But people occasionally use it in exactly the same sense as regardless. This non-word has probably come about through a confusion with 'irrespective' and/or a desire to create a more emphatic form of regardless.

REGRETFUL or REGRETTABLE

These two adjectives, with their connections to remorse and sadness, are sometimes confused in their applications.

Regretful relates only to people, and means 'capable of showing' 'regret':

✓ The defendant claimed to be regretful over what he had done.

Regrettable applies to incidents or situations (but not directly to people) which are 'causing regret':

✓ Then, in a regrettable turn of events, the company decided to close the factory.

The same distinction applies to the adverbs:

✓ Regrettably, credit card debt is also the most widely available...

Regretful doesn't mean causing regret.

REIGN or REIN

To **reign** is to 'rule over'.

To **rein** is to 'control with reins' (used of a horse, young child, etc.) but it is most often used figuratively with 'in' to mean 'restrain':
- ✓ But the Pakistanis have done little so far to rein in the thousands of Taliban operating from Baluchistan.

RELIABLE or RELIANT

Reliable describes a person or system or object which can be relied on, and carries the sense of 'dependable', 'trustworthy':
- ✓ He is a very reliable person and he will never let you down.

Reliant (followed by 'on') applies to the people who do the relying and so means 'dependent'.

RESPECTIVE or IRRESPECTIVE

Respectively has a function here as it makes clear which thing takes which role. But the word is often used unnecessarily.

Irrespective means 'without regard to':
- ✓ Everyone else has to share out anything left over, irrespective of age and seniority.

RESTFUL, RESTIVE or RESTLESS

Restful means 'soothing', 'tranquil', and is applied, not to people, but to experiences that may have a calming effect.

There is more than a shade of difference between the adjectives **restive** and **restless**. This latter word means simply 'unable to stay still'; unlike restive it does not imply that anyone is attempting to exercise control.

RING or WRING

To **wring** has several meanings, including to 'twist' (as in, wring one's hands) and to 'exact' (wring a confession from someone).

Ring, too, has a range of meanings from 'encircle' to 'call on the telephone'.

RISKY or RISQUE

These two words, one English, one French, amount to the same thing.
Risky means 'dangerous':
- ✓ The turpentine road was a risky drive.

Risque—generally with an acute accent on the 'e'—comes from the French *risquer*, which translates as 'risk'. This word is only used in a sexual context.

S

SANCTION or SANCTIONS

As a verb **to sanction** means to 'give permission'. It is a formal word.
Actually, the singular noun sanction can mean 'permission or 'approval'—but, in practice, **sanctions** is almost exclusively used in the plural to describe the 'formal penalties' which follow from some infringement of laws or rules, as in economic sanctions that are being imposed.

SHALL or WILL

The distinction between the two is that, when all that is being expressed is simple futurity, shall 'should' be used with the first person singular and plural (I/we) and will with the second and third persons (you/he/she/they):

I/we shall see you tomorrow.
- ✓ You/he/she/they will be at the station on time.

The shall/will link with particular pronouns is reversed when the sentence contains an element of compulsion or intention or determination: in short, anything that makes it more than a simple statement about the future. In these cases the first person (I/we) takes will while the others are followed by shall:
- ✓ 'I will do it, and there's no way you can stop me!'

✓ 'You shall go to the library' said the teacher.

SHEAR or SHEER

To **shear** is to 'clip' (as in sheep-shearing) and to 'cut'.
The adjective **sheer** means 'downright', 'absolute'.
As a verb to sheer means to 'swerve', 'turn from':
   ✓ He came prepared for a confrontation but sheered away from one at the last moment.

SHOO-IN or SHOE-IN

A **shoo-in**—the term was US slang originally and derives from a rigged horse race is the 'inevitable winner of a race', a 'sure thing'.
Shoe-in is associated with fitting and shoehorns.

SHOULD or WOULD

The difference between these two verb forms follows that for 'shall/will'.
Should can be used for the first person singular or plural:
   ✓ I/we should like to thank the speaker.
While **would** is appropriate for other pronouns:
   ✓ You/he/she/they would have arrived by now but for the traffic jam.
Should be used when the meaning of 'ought to' is intended:
   ✓ You really should try and see it.

SIMPLE or SIMPLISTIC

Simple has a range of meanings from the positive ('plain', 'unpretentious') to the negative ('gullible', 'silly').
Simplistic means 'naive', 'oversimplified' and is almost always used in a critical sense. A simple plan may be a good one precisely because of its simplicity but a simplistic plan can never be good because it fails to take account of the complexities of a situation.

SITTING or SAT

Sat is increasingly used where better English would demand sitting.

People were described as **sitting** round a table while a baby might be sat in its high chair. In other words, to be **sat** is to be put in your position (either by being directed to it or by being physically lifted onto a seat).

SOMETIME or SOME TIME

The single word **sometime** is an adverb, meaning 'at an unspecified or unknown point in time':
- ✓ 'Come up and see me sometime' was the minister's catch phrase.

As an adjective sometime means 'former':
- ✓ She was a sometime magistrate and mayor of the town.

Some time (two words, adjective + noun) means 'for a period of time', usually quite a long period:
- ✓ For some time now we've been thinking of going for a holiday in Spain.

STATIONARY or STATIONERY

The endings of these words are pronounced the same, and it is easy to put the wrong one. A classic confusable.

Stationary (adjective only) means 'not moving':
- ✓ The train remained stationary.

Stationery (noun only) defines the paper, pens, etc. used in a workplace.

STIGMA or STIGMATA

A **stigma** is a 'mark of shame or disgrace', although the word is generally used less intensely.

The plural version of the word, **stigmata**, is only found in a religious context since it refers to 'the five wounds which Christ received on the cross' (from nails and spear).

The verb to **stigmatize**—meaning to 'brand with shame' and so to 'condemn'.

STRAIGHT or STRAIT

The adjective **straight** means 'direct', 'without a curve' and so by extension, honest'. The noun use is mostly found in a racing context and in the singular.

Another principal noun (and adjectival) use is a slang or informal one to mean 'heterosexual'.

Strait is an adjective meaning 'narrow', 'confining', and is now used only as part of a couple of longer words, straitjacket and straitlaced.

As a noun, almost always in the plural, strait(s) describes 'a narrow stretch of water between two seas' or has the sense of 'difficult circumstances', often with 'dire' in front of it:

✓ After the theft they found themselves in dire financial straits.

STRATEGY or TACTICS

Strategy has long since moved from its origins as a word of war (where it means 'generalship', 'campaign planning') and now encompasses any 'large-scale and long-term planning'. In the 1990s especially it became a favourite term in education and the 'soft' sciences, producing expressions such as 'classroom strategies', 'learning strategies', etc.

Tactics—very often used in the plural—underpin strategy, that is, they are the 'means to reach a goal', the detailed manoeuvres that enable a strategic plan to be realized.

SUGGESTIBLE or SUGGESTIVE

Two terms connected to suggestion but with widely different uses. Both are slightly pejorative.

Suggestible means 'open to suggestion' and so 'gullible' or 'easily influenced'.

But **suggestive** generally defines comments which contain a double meaning or have a sexual undertone.

T

TAIL or TALE

A **tail** is the 'posterior extremity of an animal'. In cricket, tail describes the players who are put on to bat at the end.

A **tale** is a 'story', often one which is spoken rather than written down and sometimes with overtones of childhood. It can be true or fictitious or just plain malicious in the sense of 'telling tales'.

TEMERITY or TIMIDITY

These two nouns are opposites.

Temerity means 'daring', with the suggestion of rashness. It is more usually applied to, say, challenges to authority than cases of physical daring. **Timidity** points to an opposite attitude: 'lack of nerve', a shyness that makes its possessor unassertive:

✓ Timidity made him reluctant to speak out even when his own interests were being threatened.

THEIR, THERE or THEY'RE

Their is the possessive form of the pronoun 'they'—indicating something that belongs to 'them':

✓ They wanted the cash to begin a business.

There is an adverb of place ('over there') or is used to start a sentence or introduce certain verbs (especially 'to be'):

✓ 'There were moments when we were in real trouble.'

THROES or THROWS

Throes (always found in the plural and nearly always preceded by 'in the') are 'spasms' or 'pangs of pain'—they were originally birth pangs. The word retains something of this old meaning.

✓ The country is in the throes of inflation.

Throes shouldn't be confused with **throws,** plural of the noun throw ('casting', 'act of throwing', 'a loose covering').

TITILLATE or TITIVATE

To **titillate** is to 'tickle', to 'mildly excite', almost always with a sexual application.

The similarity in sound between titillate and **titivate**—or an artificial emphasis on the first syllable of the second word—may suggest a sexual meaning here too, but in fact titivate is to 'tidy', to 'make smarter':

- ✓ I want them to think well of me and the office. So I have been going round tidying and titivating.

TORPID or TORRID

Torpid means 'sluggish':

- ✓ The hot weather made the animals torpid.

Torrid means 'scorching', 'parched':

- ✓ The torrid climate meant we couldn't go out during the day.

(The most usual application of torrid is in its associated sense of 'hot with passion'. Others include 'sensual', 'explicit', 'frank', and the old favourite 'steamy'.)

TORTUOUS or TORTUROUS

Tortuous means 'twisting' or 'highly complicated':

- ✓ We almost got lost on the tortuous mountain path.

Torturous derives from torture, and means 'causing severe physical or mental pain':

- ✓ I spent a torturous hour in the traffic jam.

TRAVELLER or TOURIST

Two words which mean almost the same thing but which carry different overtones.

A **traveller** is 'one who travels' (and the term also has the specialized sense of 'travelling salesman or saleswoman'). There's a sense of purpose to the word, as in 'business traveller', and often of adventure. Bookshops and newspapers have travel, not tourist, sections.

A **tourist** is 'one who travels for pleasure', a 'sightseer'. There's sometimes a touch of criticism in the word, particularly in a phrase such as 'health tourist', which implies travelling with the sole purpose of taking advantage of some facility or amenity of a country.

TRIUMPHANT TRIUMPHAL or TRIUMPHALIST

Triumphant means 'rejoicing in victory', and generally applies to individuals, teams, etc. and their words and reactions after they've won:

The team was triumphant after their fifth victory in a row.

Triumphal describes rather the process of 'commemorating a victory'.

TROOPER or TROUPER

A **trooper** is a 'private soldier/a jawan'.

A **trouper** is 'someone who plays in a troupe of actors or other performers'.

TRUSTEE or TRUSTY

A **trustee**—pronounced to sound the double 'ee'—is a 'person who is entrusted with managing property or an organization' (often for charitable purposes).

A **trusty** is a 'person in jail who has earned special privileges' (usually through good behaviour).

U

UNDERLIE or UNDERLAY

To **underlie** is to 'lie beneath'.

To **underlay** is to 'lay under'—i.e. to 'place something underneath something else'.

USE or UTILIZE

Utilize suggests an active putting to use of whatever one can find:
- ✓ Robinson Crusoe utilized the resources of his desert island.

Use is a plainer term:
- ✓ She used her knowledge of languages to get along with people.

Utilize is often used because use doesn't sound sufficiently weighty.

V

VALUABLE or INVALUABLE

The 'in-' prefix to invaluable sometimes causes people to assume it is the negative form of valuable (probably by analogy with 'incorrect', 'indecisive', etc.).

The opposite of **valuable** ('having worth') is 'valueless' or 'worthless'. People may occasionally use **invaluable** in this second sense, but its correct meaning is 'not capable of being valued' or 'beyond price'—and therefore very valuable indeed. It tends not to be applied to objects.

VENAL, VENIAL or VERNAL

Venal means 'open to being bribed' and so 'corrupt'.

Venial, usually used with 'sin' or 'offence', means 'forgivable'.
Neither word should be confused with **vernal**, meaning 'connected to spring'.

W

WAIVE, WAVE, WAVER or WAIVER

To **waive** is to 'forgo', to 'hold back from claiming an entitlement'.

A **waiver** (noun only) is the 'act of waiving' or, more usually, a 'document which shows this', that is, it indicates that the possessor is exempt from some fee or charge.

Wave has a variety of meanings including to 'signal' and to 'move in an undulating way'.

WASTE or WASTAGE

As a noun or verb **waste** characterizes activities which are extravagant or useless (a waste of money, to waste time) while the adjective waste describes anything which is 'unused' or 'rejected' (waste ground, waste paper).

Wastage refers to 'inevitable loss through use or decay'.

WEATHER, WHETHER or WETHER

Weather is 'atmosphere', sun, rain, etc.

Whether is a conjunction introducing the first of one or more alternatives (whether... or).

A **wether** is a 'castrated ram'.

A **bell-wether**—which can be male or female—is the leading sheep in a flock, followed by the others because it has a bell hung round its neck.

WHISKY or WHISKEY

Two drinks with a certain amount in common, and a one-letter difference.

The standard English spelling of **whisky** (i.e. the stuff distilled in Scotland) doesn't have an 'e'.

But the **whiskey** which is produced in Ireland or America takes the 'e' (and this is the standard US spelling).

WHO or WHICH

Who is used for individuals:
- ✓ The man who broke the bank at Delhi...

Which tends to be for events, objects, etc.:
- ✓ There was a historic battle which took place on this spot.

WHO'S or WHOSE

Who's is the contracted form of who is. **Whose** is the possessive form of who. Although the words sound the same they have completely different functions.

WILE, WHILE or WHILST

As a noun **wile** describes a 'trick', but there's often something pleasant or seductive about it.

To **wile**, a rare verb, also means to 'trick' or 'beguile'.

Wile has nothing to do with **while**—or **whilst**.

WINNIN or WINSOME

Winning, apart from its sense of victorious (the winning team), can mean 'engaging' or 'persuasive': a **winning** smile, a winning speech.

Winsome has absolutely nothing to do with 'win'. Although it can carry the sense of 'attractive', it is almost always used in contexts which suggest something rather 'cute and calculated'.

WREAK, WRECK or REEK

To **wreak** is to 'bring about harm', to 'inflict vengeance':
  ✓ Wherever the cyclone went, it wreaked a trail of havoc.
To **wreck,** on the other hand, is to 'destroy', or to 'spoil something so completely as to put it out of action'.
To **reek** is to 'give off smoke or fumes' and generally applies to unpleasant smells or, metaphorically, to anything unattractive or corrupt.
  ✓ I don't like garlic because it reeks.

YIN or YANG

Yin and **yang** are Chinese terms describing the complementary (but opposed) principles which underlie religion, medicine and so on.
Yang is the 'active male principle', light and warm, while **yin** is the colder and more passive 'feminine principle', each necessary to the other, held in a state of balance and tension, etc.

YOKE or YOLK

The noun **yoke** is 'anything that joins items/people/animals together', with a verb meaning of 'link'. In a concrete sense the yoke is a 'frame that fits round the neck' (of oxen, for example) and, metaphorically, it can also stand as a 'symbol of oppression or slavery'.
Yolk is the 'yellow part of an egg'.

YOUNG or YOUTHFUL

Both words mean roughly the same, but using **youthful**, despite its being a positive term, could cause mild offence in the wrong context.
Young tends carries overtones of 'fresh and vigorous'. It's quite often used not about the young (who are naturally youthful) but about older people who've retained—or clung onto—the habits,

attitudes, etc. of earlier days. If you describe someone as having a youthful appearance the implication is that they look younger than they are, often surprisingly so.

YOUR or YOU'RE

Your is the possessive form of the pronoun 'you':
- ✓ Don't forget your toothbrush.

You're is the shortened form of 'you are':
- ✓ You're not going to believe this!

Z

ZENITH or NADIR

The **zenith** is the 'position in the sky directly over the observer's head', and so comes to mean 'high point', 'most flourishing period'.

The **nadir** is the 'direct opposite of the zenith', and if taken literally would apply to the position under the observer's feet, or rather the 'lowest point', the 'worst period'.

Part II

A

Abdabs or **habdabs** is a state of extreme nervousness or the jitters.

Abdomen is straight from Latin and originally denoted the fat deposited around the belly.

Aberuncator; to aberuncate is to pull up by the roots or extirpate.

To **ablaqueate** is to expose the roots of a tree by loosening or removing soil.

Ablatitious means 'diminishing, lessening' a vowel change in related words—e.g. sing, sang, sung—is called an **ablaut** (from German *ab*, 'off', and *Laut*, 'sound') or **gradation**.

To **ablocate** means to rent or rent out.

Abnegate means renounce or reject something desired or valuable.

Abnormal means 'not normal, different from normal' while **subnormal** means 'below normal'.

To **abraid** is to awake, arouse, or startle.

An **abreuvoir** is a space between bricks or masonry.

To **abvolate** is to fly away.

Acalculia is the inability to perform simple arithmetic.

Acatery are things bought or a storeroom for provisions, respectively.

To **accerse** is to summon.

Accismus is the pretended refusal of something that is actually coveted.

An **acclivity** is an upward slope.

Acclumsid is 'numb, paralyzed; clumsy'.

Acedia is spiritual sluggishness, indifference, or apathy.

Acedolagnia is complete indifference to sex.

An **acephalist** is someone who does not acknowledge a superior.

Acheron is another name for infernal regions or a river in Hell.

The original notion contained in the word **acid** is 'pointedness'.

Acrasia is acting against your better judgement or a lack of self-control.

Acrohypothermy is cold feet.

An ingrown nail is an **acronyx**.

An **actioner** is an exciting action-and-adventure film.

The word '**actor**' is preferred now for both men and women; **actor** was originally an agent or administrator and in Latin it meant 'doer'.

Acturience is the desire for or impulse to act.

Acuity pertains principally to hearing, vision, understanding, and wit.

Acumen suggests that keenness relates to a person's mind, whereas **acuity** suggests that is relates to a person's performance; **acumen** is something that a person has, whereas **acuity** is something that a person displays.

Adagio is music played 'at ease'.

Adidas is a blend of the first syllables of Adolf (Adi) Dassler, inventor of these athletic shoes.

Adnexa are the parts adjoining a human organ.

Adoxography is good writing on a trivial subject.

Adret is a mountain slope which faces the sun; the opposite is **ubac**.

An **aedicule** is a small room or structure used as a shrine—or a niche for a statue.

Aerometry is the measurement of airflow through the nose and mouth during speech.

Affluential is a blend of affluent and influential.

An **agape** is a love feast.

Agathism is the belief that things tend to work out for the better.

Agathokakological means 'made of good and evil'.

An **agelast** is a person who never laughs.

Agennesis is another word for impotence.

Agminate means 'grouped together in a cluster'.

Agnail is actually the torn skin around a fingernail (from Old High German *ungnagel*).

Agnoilogy is the branch of philosophy studying human ignorance.

Agomphosis/agomphiasis is looseness of teeth.

Agrostology is the study of grasses.

Agrypnia is a synonym for insomnia; a fit of shivering is **ague**.

Akrasia is weakness of will (Greek o, 'without,' and *krator*, 'power') when someone acts against their better judgement through weakness of will.

An **alector** is a person who is unable to sleep (from Homer's *Odyssey*).

Algesia is sensitiveness to pain.

Alieniloquy is a word for rambling or evasive talk.

Alimentotherapy is the assignment of dietary therapy to treat a disease.

Allodoxaphobia is a fear of others' opinions.

An **allograph** is a signature or writing done for another person.

If your feet are growing faster than your body as a whole, they are **allometric**.

Allopathy is treatment to suppress the symptoms of illness using the principle of opposites while **homeopathy** encourages rather than suppresses the body's reaction to an illness.

Allusion is an 'indirect mention,' **illusion** is 'false impression,' and **delusion** is 'deception' which is much stronger than **illusion**.

Alogy is unreasonableness or absurdity.

Aloha is Hawaiian for both hello and goodbye and also means 'love'.

Alpenglow is the rosy lighting or the setting or rising sun as seen on high mountains.

Altoids (the breath mint) is from Latin *altus*, 'highest, best,' and *–oid*, an older pharmaceutical suffix.

Amalgamate seems to go back to Greek *malagma*, 'softening'.

Amazon.com was so named because its founder wanted the store's inventory to be as deep and wide as the Amazon River.

Ambassador is based on Latin *ambactus*, 'servant'.

An **ambodexter** is an unethical lawyer or bribed juror.

Amentia is being out of one's mind with joy, in a rapturous daze.

Amiture is another word for friendship.

Amok is from a Malay *amuk*, 'fighting furiously' or 'rushing in a frenzy'.

Among applies to things that can be separated and counted; **amid** to things that cannot.

Amphoric or **amphorous** is hollow-sounding, 'like the sound made by blowing across the top of an open bottle'.

Anaconda comes from a Sinhalese term for 'whip snake'.

An **analysand** is a person undergoing psychoanalysis.

Analysis is from Greek elements meaning 'loosen up'.

Anarchy is from Greek *anarkhos*, 'without a chief'.

Anaudia is loss of voice.

Anguria is a gourd or watermelon.

If one is **anhelous,** one is short of breath or panting.

Ankylosis is stiffness or immobility in a joint.

One's **anlage** is a an inherited disposition to certain traits or a particular character development; **atavism** is the reappearance of characteristic after skipping one or more generations.

An **answer-jobber** is one who makes a living of writing answers.

Anthem is ultimately an alteration of *antiphon* 'scriptural verse said or sung as a response and they started out a compositions from the Book of Psalms, then evolved to national (patriotic) anthems'.

Anthology is from Greek *anthos*, 'flower', so it is a 'bouquet' of literary pieces.

Anthropomorphism is the ascription of a human attribute or personality to anything impersonal or irrational.

Antibiotic is from *anti*, 'against, not,' and *biotikos*, 'fit for life'.

Antipastic means pertaining to appetizers or hors d'oeuvres (or the eating of them).

A word used in a sense opposite of the usual is an **antiphrasis**.

Anxiolytic means serving to reduce anxiety and **phrontifugic** is helping one escape one's thoughts or cares.

Anyway is correct if you mean 'in any case', otherwise, use **any way**.

Apositic is 'taking away the appetite'.

Appetence is desire or longing.

Appetible is a synonym for desirable.

April is from Latin *operire*, 'to open,' (*aperia*, 'open') as it is when trees unfold and the earth opens with new life.

Aprosexia is the inability to concentrate.

Aquose is a synonym for watery.

An **arborescence** is a tree-like growth or formation.

Ardent means 'burning, fiery' or 'glowing like fire'.

Armsaye or **armscye** (or **armseye** or **scye**) is the armhole in clothing, the hole in a shirt, sweater, jumper etc. through which you put your hand and arm.

Asbestos is from Greek words meaning 'unquenchable'.

Ascesis is the practice of self-discipline.

An **aspirant** is one who is seeking a higher position or some distinction.

Aspire comes (from Latin *spirare*, 'breathe') first meant 'breathe into' or 'rise, rise up'.

Aspirin comes from, German *acetylierte Spirsaure* (acetylated salicylic acid).

Asterisk comes from the Greek word *aster*, 'star,' and it can be used to describe a little star or something starlike; **asterisk** should be pronounced AS-tuh-risk.

Astrometry is the precise measurement of celestial objects.

B

Babble is based on the repeated ba-ba-ba made by a **baby** or young child; **babe** and **baby** are also probably imitative of an infant's speech.

A **backfriend** is a secret enemy, a pretended or false friend.

Backwater is water fed by the backflow of a stream or river.

Baksheesh is a small sum of money given as a tip or as alms.

Balkan is derived from a Turkish word signifying 'mountain'.

Ballet is borrowed from French 'little dance', the diminutive of *bal*, 'dance'.

Bamboo is ultimately derived from Malay *mamby*.

Banana comes from Arabic *banayna*, meaning 'finger, toes,' and bananas were once called Indian figs; the **banana** 'tree' is really a giant herb with a rhizome instead of roots and its 'trunk' is made of leaves, not wood.

Bandanna comes from Hindi *badhnu*, 'tie-dyeing, cloth so dyed'; **bandanna** is the proper spelling, though bandana is acceptable.

Barbate means 'bearded' and **barbatulous** is having a small beard.

Barber comes from Latin *barba*, 'beard,' because a **barber's** work consisted of trimming beards and originally they also performed surgery and dentistry.

Barbie's original name was Barbara, after the inventor's daughter.

Bated breath is based on the idea that the breath is abated or stopped.

Batik is Javanese, literally 'painted'.

Batter is based on a French word *bateure*, 'action of beating'.

BC means Before Christ, the years before the modern era of history, but now many use **BCE**, meaning Before Common Era; **AD** is *Latin* for Anno Domini, 'in the year of our lord' to denote time after the birth of Christ, but many now use **CE** for Common Era.

Because is from the earlier 'by cause,' in turn based on French *par cause de*, 'by reason of' and it originally meant 'arrive, come'.

A warning shock for an earthquake is a **before-shock**.

Bellboy first referred to a ship's boy who rang a bell.

Belly has its origin in *belig*, 'skin bag', which was used to carry beans and peas.

Beret is based on Latin *birrus*, 'hooded cape'.

Beriberi is a Sinhalese reduplication of *beri*, 'weakness'.

Betroth is from the elements 'be' and 'truth', as in 'be true to (somebody)'.

Betweenity is another word for indecision.

Bibliobibuli are people who read too much.

A **biblioklept** is a book thief.

Bigamy breaks down to *bi-*, 'twice' and *gamos*, 'married'.

Billet-doux, a love letter, is French for 'sweet note'.

Biscuit is Latin for *biscotum panem*, 'twice cooked bread'.

Bisque is an extra turn, point, or stroke allowed to a weaker player in croquet, court tennis, or golf.

A **blazer** was originally a brightly coloured ('blazing') jacket used in boating, cricket, and other sports.

Blog, formed by contraction of Web log (or weblog), is essentially an online personal diary or journal available to the public on a website.

Blunt originally meant 'dull, obtus, foolish'.

American humourist Gelett Burgess coined **blurb**—and he made a comic book with a character named Miss Blinda Blurb.

Bodacious is a blend of bold and audacious.

A **bodyscape** is a map of the body.

A joke that gets a hearty laugh is a **boffola**.

Bogus originally denoted a machine for making counterfeit money.

Bole is another name for the trunk of a tree.

Bombus is a buzzing in the ears, stomach, etc.

Bonbon is a French word for sweet.

Boodles is a great quantity, especially of money.

Bosh, 'nonsense, foolish talk,' is from Turkish *bos*, 'empty, worthless'.

Boss derives from the Dutch word *baas*, 'master'.

Both is from an Indo-European base meaning 'each of two'.

A **bottle** of wine is a **bottle** full of wine and a wine **bottle** is an empty **bottle** used to hold wine.

Bouquet comes from French *bosquet*, originally meaning 'a little forest' or 'clump of trees'.

Bowel derives from Latin *botelluss*, diminutive of *botulus*, 'sausage'.

Branular means pertaining to or affecting the brain.

The meat of a boar is called **brawn**.

Brazen means belonging to or made of brass.

Breakfast literally means 'breaking the fast' of the night, as it is the first meal after sleeping.

Bribe, from Old French, was originally a piece of bread given to beggars; the original sense of **bribe** is 'extort, rob'.

Brilliant can be traced to Italian *brillare*, 'shine, shining'.

When your glass or cup is filled to the brim, you have a **brimmer**.

C

Cab is a shortening of cabriolet, which took its name from French *cabriole*, 'goat's leap'—from the motion of the carriage.

The word **cabinet** originally meant a small room, and it came to apply to the group of politicians who met in the room.

To **cabobble** is to mystify, puzzle, or confuse.

Caboose originally signified the kitchen on merchant ships or fishing boats, having come from Dutch *kabuis*, 'ship's gallery'.

Cache first meant 'a hiding place'.

Cachexia is a chronically bad outlook or way of thinking.

Cacographgy is bad handwriting or poor spelling.

Cacology is a bad choice of words or (poor pronunciation).

A **caconym** is a 'bad name' or 'bad terminology'.

Cacophemism is the opposite of **euphemism**.

Caducity means 'senility,' 'frailty,' or 'transitory nature'.

Café is French for both coffee and coffee house.
Cafeteria is literally Latin American Spanish for 'coffee shop, coffeehouse'.
Caffeine literally means 'something found in coffee'.
Cakewalk started out as a competitive dance and the winner of the **cakewalk** got a cake as a prize.
A person who draws with crayons is a **calcographer**.
Calculate comes from *calculus*, 'a pebble used for counting and calculating'.
Calid is another way of saying 'warm, tepid'.
Calisthenics comes from Greek *cali-*, 'beauty, especially elegant' and *sthenos* 'strong'.
Calligraphy is from Greek meaning 'beautiful writing'.
Callus is a hard patch of skin; **callous** is an adjective meaning 'indifferent to suffering' or 'hardened'.
Camcorder is a blend of video camera and video recorder.
Camisole derives from a diminutive of Latin *camisia*, 'shirt or nightgown'.
Camouflage derives from French *camou-flet*, 'a puff of smoke'.
Campus is 'field' in Latin.
Can applies to what is possible and **may** to what is permissible; **can** means 'able to,' **may** means 'permitted to'.
Canapé is French for 'couch, mosquito-netted sofa' or 'covering' and is bread upon which other items sit on for their being served before dinner.
Candid comes from Latin *candidus*, 'white' and first meant 'pure, innocent'; **candidate** is based on the same Latin word, and became Latin *candidatus*, 'white-robed' as the traditional attire of a **candidate** for office was a white toga because it symbolised honesty.
Candle is from Latin *candere*, 'to be white or glisten, to shine'.
Candy comes into English from Arabic *qandi*, 'sugar,' which may be related to Sanskrit *khandokah*, 'sugar in crystalline pieces' or *khanda*, 'broken piece' applied to sugar pieces broken off a large block of crystallized sugar.

Canister comes from a word related to cane and originally was a basket for bread, fruit, or flowers.

A small can is a **cannikin**; a small pan is a **pannikin**.

Clinic first meant 'teaching of medicine at the bedside'.

Clinker is a stonelike furnace or coal residue.

Clinomania is an excessive desire to stay in bed.

Clo is the unit of measurement for the thermal insulation value of clothing.

Close, from Latin *clausum*, 'closed place, first meant enclosure'.

Closet first denoted a private or small room.

Cloud from Old English *clud* meant hill or rock at first, the name of a cloud describes both its appearance and its height above the ground.

A **cloudburst** is a torrential local downpour of rain of short duration.

Clout once meant 'heavy blow'.

Clown may derive from Northern Frisian meaning 'clumsy fellow' or clod and it first referred to an unrefined person.

A **clutch** is a group of eggs laid in a single session.

Coal originally meant a glowing piece of wood or a cinder.

The difference between a **coast** and the **shore** is the **coast** is the seaward limit of the land and the **shore** is the landward limit of the sea.

The original senses of **coax** were fondle, pet or make a simpleton of.

Cobra is from Portuguese *cobra de capello*, 'snake with hood' based on Latin *colubra*, 'snake'.

Coca-Cola is from *Quecha kuka*, 'coca leaves, coca bush,' borrowed via Spanish coca + cola from languages of West Africa *kola*, 'cola nut'.

Cockcrow is a literary word for dawn.

To **cockerate** is to brag.

A candy heart with a message is called a **cockle**.

In **cocksure**, cock is an euphemism for 'God'.

Cocktail as drink sense for an 'adulterated' spirit.

If your Adam's apple is larger than normal, you are **cock-throppled**.

Cocoa is an alteration of Spanish *cacao*.

Coconut it the nut or seed of the coco-palm, from Portuguese *coco*, literally, 'bogeyman,' from the resemblance of a **coconut** to a grotesque head.

An egg cooked in water just below boiling is **coddled**.

A **codger** is a mildly eccentric person.

Codicil is a diminutive of *codex*, a 'small part of a legal document,' usually used to add to or change something about a larger piece of writing.

Coerce derives from Latin *arcere*, 'restrain'.

A **coffered** ceiling is one with ornamental sunken panels in a box like structure.

Coffin is French for 'little basket', from Greek *kophinos*, 'basket,' and first generally meant 'box, case, casket, chest'.

Cogitabund is being deep in thought.

Cognac is named for a town in western France.

A blood relative is a **cognate**.

Cognomen is literally 'name by which one is known'.

Coin comes from the wedge-shaped tool or dye (Latin *cuneus*, 'wedge') that was used to hammer or stamp pieces of money.

Coincide can mean 'occupy the same portion of space'.

A word inventor is a **coiner** or **neologist**.

Coir is the fibre from the outer husk of a coconut.

A **col** is an area of low pressure between two high-pressure systems.

Cola is from Temne *k'ola*, '**cola** nut', cola seeds are used to make **Coca-Cola** and Pepsi-**Cola**.

When the moon is far to the north it is popularly called a **cold** moon.

Cold-blooded (*poikilothermic, poikilothermal*) is used for creatures whose blood takes on the temperature of their environment; **warm-blooded** (*homoiothrmic, homeothermal*) is having a fairly steady body temperature governed by the thermotaxic nerve mechanism.

Cold-fire is fuel laid for a fire, but unlit.

Beetle specialists are **coleopterists**.

Colic is, literally, 'pertaining to the colon'.

Collapse is a back-formation of collapsed.

Collar descends from Latin *collum*, 'neck'.

Collate first meant 'to bring together for comparison; compare copies carefully' before it meant 'put together sheets to make two or more copies of a document'.

A **colleague** is literally 'one chosen or delegated to be or work with another' and comes via French from Latin *collega* (*com-* 'with' and *leg-* 'choose').

The word **college** comes from Latin *collegium*, Legium, association, partnership, from college, partner in office. The word **university** is from Latin *universitas*, 'the whole' from *universus*, 'combined into one'. The difference between a **college** and a **university** is that a **college** offers degrees in one or a few specific areas, while a **university** is a collection of colleges.

Collegial is the adjective for colleague.

Colletic means adhesive or adhesive substance.

Collocate is to place side by side.

Colloquial is Latin *col* and *loqui*, 'speak' and it describes a term used in ordinary or informal conversation.

Colloquy is a conversation (from Latin *colloquium*).

Collywobbles is a humorous term for stomach pain, queasiness, intense anxiety, or nervousness (from colic + wobble).

Cologne was created in **Cologne**, Germany and first called **Eau-de-Cologne** or **Cologne** water.

A **colon** (from Greek meaning 'limb, member or clause of sentence') introduces a part of a sentence that exemplifies, elaborates, balances, or undermines the preceding part.

Colon the greater portion of the large intestine, comes from Greek *kolon*, 'food meat'.

Colonel comes from the Italian *colonna*, 'column', from the arrangement of troops who were led by the head officer of a **regiment**; in Spanish it was *coronel* and it was so spelled in English at first and pronounced KORR-o-nel.

Colour refers to the wavelength composition of light; **shade** is a gradation of colour referring to its degree of darkness; **tint** is a gradation referring to its degree of lightness; and **hue** indicates a modification of a basic colour.

Baby seahorses are called **colts**.

Coma derives from Greek words translating to 'lying down in bed.'

Comb comes from *gombhos* (pre-Teutonic) for teeth, as the first combs were dried backbones or jawbones of fish.

A **comediographer** is a writer of comedies.

If something is tending to produce or aggravate acne, it is **comedogenic**.

Comedy comes from Greek *komos*, literally meaning 'village bard or village merrymaker'.

Comely is from a Dutch word *komlick*, fitting.

Come-on was first a slang term for a con man or swindler.

Comets, which have tails, get their name from Greek *kometes*, 'long-haired star'.

Comfort is from Latin *con*, 'an intensifier', and *fortis*, 'strong'.

Comical is 'funny unintentionally'.

Comma (from Greek 'a piece cut off') first meant a short clause or phrase within a sentence—and then came to be the name for the punctuation mark.

Commence is based on Latin *con-* (for emphasis) and *initiare*, 'begin'.

Commerce is another word for conversation.

Committee's original meaning was an individual to whom some charge, function, or trust is committed.

Commode is another word for toilet.

Commodity first meant 'convenience, suitability' and then a 'person's benefit, convenience, interest' and its Latin root meant 'due measure, fitness, convenience, complaisance'.

A **commonplace** book is a personal journal in which quotable passages, literary excerpts, and comments are written.

A **commorient** is a person killed in a disaster that claimed other lives.

Commuter came to mean any regular traveller to work.

Compact (adjective) can mean made up or composed of.

Companion is from French *compagnon*, 'one who eats bread with another' from Latin *com*, 'with' and *panis*, 'bread'.

A **companionway** is a stairway or ladder from a deck to the cabin below.

A **compare** is an equal or a rival.

A **compartment** describes a watertight division of a ship.

Compass (noun) first meant 'cunning, cleverness, ingenuity'.

Compathy is shared feeling.

Compendious means 'abridged, succinct not voluminous'.

Compete comes from Latin *competere*, 'come together', but in later Latin it developed the sense strive together, which was the basis for the English term.

Competent once meant appropriate, suitable.

Competitiveness refers to an abstract quality, whereas **competition** implies a practical activity whose manifestation can be observed.

Compital means 'pertaining to a crossroads'.

Complacent means 'pleased or satisfied with how things are, with how they effect one's self'; **complaisant** means 'attempting or eager to please or satisfy', 'obliging, affable'. **Complacent** thus refers to a state of mind and **complaisant** to a disposition to behave or conduct oneself in a way that pleases or satisfies others.

Complain is from Latin meaning 'to beat the breast' or 'to lament'.

Complement is 'to complete, round out' and **compliment** is 'to praise or admire' and as a noun it is an expression of praise or admiration.

Complicate, from Latin *plicare*, 'fold', first meant 'fold together, entangle, intertwine'.

Component specifically implies that it is part of a machine or vehicle.

Deportment adds the sense of action or activity to a mode of conduct or behaviour; **Comportment** ('behaviour or bearing')

Compotation is another word for drinking session or drinking together.

A **compotator** is a drinking companion.

Compound meaning 'combine' comes from Latin *componere*, 'put together'; **compound,** the enclosure is from Malay *kam-pong*, 'group of buildings; village' and comes through Portuguese or Dutch.

Comprehend literally means 'seize with the senses'.

Comprise means literally 'embrace'. A zoo comprises mammals, reptiles, and birds (because it 'embraces' or includes them) but animals do not **comprise** (embrace) a zoo, they **constitute** a zoo.

Compromise started literally as a joint promise.

Comptroller is an erroneous spelling of controller; **comptroller** should be pronounced Kuhn-TROH-luhr.

A **Comprise compurgator** is a sworn witness to the innocence or good character of a person.

Compursion is wrinkling one's face.

Computeracy is a blend of computer literacy.

Confetti is the plural of Italian *confetto*, 'small sweet' as this was originally real or imitation bon-bons thrown during carnival or after a wedding.

In **confide** and **confident**, part of the word is from Latin *fidere*, 'trust'.

Configure first meant 'fashion according to a model'.

Confirm first meant 'make firm or firmer'.

Confit is duck or other meal cooked slowly in its own fat.

One who confesses is a **confitent**.

Congeal (become semi-solid, especially upon cooling) is from Latin *con*, 'together' and *gelare*, 'freeze'.

Congee is water in which rice has been boiled.

Congenial first meant kindered or sharing the same disposition.

Congenital means existing from birth while hereditary is 'transmitted from one generation to another'.

Congestion in the body is an accumulation of fluid.

Congratulate's etymology is *con-* and Latin *gratulari*, 'manifest one's joy' and first meant to 'celebrate with some act'.

Conifer literally is Latin meaning 'cone-bearing'.

Another name for pink eye is **conjunctivitis**.

Cenjure comes from Latin words meaning 'band together by an oath, conspire'; it can also mean to beg or implore.

Conky is anybody with a big nose.

Connatural means 'innate, belonging inherently or naturally to'.

Connoisseur in French meant 'knower, judge' and it indicates an expert in a particular area whose recognized knowledge and good taste have established his/her reputation.

Consensus came into English in a physiological 'sense a set of organs' or the 'involuntary or reflex actions of the nervous system'.

Connotation is from Latin *connotare*, 'mark in addition'.

Connubial is a synonym for 'married, wedded'.

Conscience is the noun meaning a 'sense of right and wrong' while **conscious** is the adjective meaning 'aware of something, being awake'.

Consecrate's root is Latin *sacer*, 'sacred'.

Consecutive derives from Latin *consecut*, 'follow closely'.

A **consuetude** is a social custom or convention.

A **consulate** is essentially a junior embassy.

Contaminate seems to come from the base *tag*, 'touch', which became Latin *contagmen*, 'contact', and then Latin *contagmen*.

Conte is another word for adventure story.

Contemporary can be predicated of persons, conditions, or events; **contemporaneous** is predicable only of occurrences or events.

Contempt is a more engaged, more involved feeling of disapproval than disdain.

Contemptible means deserving contempt, while **contemptuous** means bestowing contempt; the first sense of contemptuous was 'despising law and order'.

Content comes from the Latin plural *contenta*, 'things contained'.

Contentment first referred to payment of a claim which 'satisfied' the obligation.

Contiguous implies having contact on all or most of one side.

Continent is 'able to control the bowels and bladder' or 'exercising self-restraint'.

Contingent suggests the possibility of happening but stresses uncertainty and dependence on other future events for existence or occurrence.

A **contour** line on a map passes through points of equal elevation or depth.

Contradict is from Latin *contra dicere*, 'speak against'.

Contralto is the voice intermediate between soprano and tenor.

Contrast was first used as a term in fine art; on a TV or computer monitor, it is a control that increases or decreases the difference between the dark and light areas of the screen.

Contrite is 'bruised, crushed' or 'worn or broken by rubbing'.

Contrive was once *controve*, from Latin *contropare*, 'represent metaphorically'.

Control first meant 'to check or verify accounts' and referred to a duplicate or keeping a copy; a **control** is the standard comparison in a statistical analysis or scientific experiment.

Contubernal is a tentmate or a person you live with, as an intimate companion.

Contusion comes from Latin *come* (intensive) and *tundere*, 'beat, hit'.

Conundrum first meant 'whim' and then 'pun' and then its current sense of 'puzzling problem', the plural is **conundra**.

Copious comes from Latin *copia*, 'plenty' (as in cornucopia).

A **corbel** is a projection of stone, brick, timber, iron, etc., jutting out from the face of a wall to support something.

The notion behind **coppice** (dense growth of bushes) is of 'cutting' and it comes from Greek *kolaphas*, 'blow', which became Latin *colpare*, 'cut'.

Copra is the dried meat of the coconut.

A **copula** is a connecting word, especially forms of 'be' linking a subject and complement.

Corrupt comes from Latin *corrumpere*, 'destroy completely' and first meant 'to destroy or spoil the flesh, fruit, or organic matter by dissolution or decomposition'.

Cortex is a Latin word meaning bark; to **coruscate** is to give forth intermittent or vibratory flashes of light, to shine with a quivering light—as light does between the trees as one drives along a road.

A cluster of ivy berries or grapes is a **corymb**.

Coryza is a head cold.

Co-sleeping is when parents allow a child to sleep in their bed.

Cosmetics comes from Greek *kosmetikos*, 'skilled in decorating', from *kosmein*, 'arrange, adorn'.

Cosmolatry or **physitism** is the worship of nature.

Cosmos is from Greek *kosmos*, 'order of world' and is often used to suggest an orderly or harmonious universe.

A **costa** is a rib or rib-like structure.

Cost-benefit refers to assessing the benefits of an undertaking in relation to its cost.

Cost-effective is anything effective and productive in relation to its cost.

Costermonger is, literally, apple dealer. A kinder word for constipation or causing constipation is **costive**.

Costume and **custom** were actually two forms of the same Latin root *consuetudinem*, 'habit, custom', with **costume** first meaning 'manners and customs belonging to a particular time and place'.

Something that **costs** a particular amount literally 'stands at or with' that price (Latin *constare*, 'to be settled or fixed, stand at a price, **cost**').

Cot is ultimately derived from Sanskrit *khatva*, 'bedstead, couch, hammock', then Hindi *khat*, and was first a small cottage or humble dwelling.

A **cote** is a shelter for birds or mammals.

A **coterie,** from French, is literally 'tenants holding land together' and now a circle of persons who associate with one another, as distinguished from 'outsiders'; a **coterie** is also a group of prairie dogs occupying a communal burrow.

Cotton is actually from Arabic *qutun*.

Cough is of onomatopoeic origin.

Coulrophobia is the fear of clowns.

Council comes from Latin words meaning 'summon' and 'together'.

Counsel is 'advice, guidance' and a **counsel** is a lawyer; a **council** is a deliberative body of people assembled for some purpose and members are **councillors**.

Coup was first a blow or stroke, from Greek *kolaphos*, 'blow with the fist'.

A **coupe** is defined as a closed, two-door, two-seat motor car and is short for French *carosse coupe*, 'shortened coach'.

Coupon is French for 'piece cut off' and originally denoted detachable portion of a bond to be given in return for payment of interest; **coupon** should be pronounced KOO-pon.

Courage comes from Latin *cor*, 'heart' and denotes this as the seat of feelings.

Courbette is when a trained horse rears up and jumps forward on the hind legs.

Courier is based on Latin *currere*, 'to run'.

Court comes from Latin *cohors*, 'enclosed yard' (the yard was the central point of a farm and its building, hence for other buildings, a town, etc.) which was extended to being a crowed assembled in such a yard and then 'area enclosed by walls or buildings'.

Coward is literally French *cove*, 'tail' (from Latin *cauda*, 'tail'), + *ard*, 'tail person', because a frightened animal 'turns tail' or has its tail between its legs.

Cowl is the section of a car that holds the windshield and dashboard.

Crastin is the morrow or the day after.

To **crastine** is to put off from day to day.

Crater comes from Greek *krater*, 'mixing bowl'.

Crayon derives from French *craie*, and earlier Latin *creta*, 'chalk clay'; in art, a **crayon** is any drawing material in stick form.

Crazy goes back to a Scandinavian word *krasa*, 'broken'.

Creative was coined in association with art, not with the divine.

Crebrous means frequent.

Creed comes from Latin *credo*, 'I believe'.

Creek has the root sense 'crooked water-way' (from Old Norse *kriki*, 'crook, twist').

Corpuscular is 'of or like twilight'.

Crestfallen is an allusion to fighting cocks whose crests fall in defeat and rise in victory.

Cricket's (the game) name is derived from French *criquet*, 'goal post, wicket'.

A vehicle or ship unfit for service is a **cripple**.

Criterion comes from Greek *criterion*, 'means of judging'.

Critic and **crisis** both ultimately come from Greek *kritos*, 'judge, discern' and then *kritikos*, 'able to make judgements and one who makes judgements', which passed into Latin *criticus* and then to English **critic**.

Crochet is from French, 'little hook' (diminutive of *croc*, 'hook') which is what is used for such needlework.

Crockery gets its name from the obsolete *crocker*, 'potter'.

Crocodile is based on Greek *krokodilos*, 'worm of the stones'.

Curl is disease of plants in which the leaves or shoots are curled up and not developed perfectly.

Curriculum, from Latin *currer* 'to run' evolved into 'to run a course' and then to the full slate of courses offered for study.

Curry is from Tamil *kari*, 'sauce', as it first meant spicy sauce for wheat cakes or rice.

Cursive comes from Latin *currere*, 'to run' and it means running hand, writing in which the pen is not raised after each character.

Cursor first meant 'runner' or 'running messenger' and now it is the moving/movable indicator on a computer screen.

Cursory means 'superficial'; **cursorial** is 'pertaining or adopted to running'.

Curt is from Latin *curtus*, 'abridged, cut short'.

Cutlery includes knives but there is no association with cut, rather being from old French *coutelier*, 'cutler's art' from *countel*, 'knife'.

Cybernetics was coined in French as *cybernetique* in the 1830s but meant 'art of governing', and in English it came to mean 'theory of control and communication processes.'

Cyclone probably comes from Greek words meaning 'circle eye'; it is the general term for a storm that can be called, depending on features and where it occurs, a hurricane, typhoon, or tornado.

D

Daft first meant crazy and silly.

A horse's mother is a **dame**, dam; the father is a **sire**.

Damage comes from Latin *damnum*, '**damage** loss'.

Damp (the noun) first meant vapour, steam or 'smoke', —especially that was harmful or noxious.

Daredevil is a contraction of 'someone ready to dare the devil'.

Darling derives from 'dear'.

Daze is from Old Norse and first meant 'exhausted from cold or exertion'.

D-Day actually means 'day day', as redundancy was common in military correspondence referring to a top-secret time.

Deadline is a Civil War term for a line that marked the distance a prisoner could go before being shot on sight.

A **deadlock** was first a lock with no spring catch.

In **deadpan**, pan means 'face'.

Deal first meant a part, portion, or division of a whole.

Dean comes from Latin *decanum*, 'chief of a group of ten', and Greek *dekanos*, 'a monk or dignitary in charge of ten others'.

Dearth means 'scarcity', not complete lack.

To **deasil** is to travel in the direction of the sun.

Death means 'act or process of dying', much the same as birth and strength were formed.

Debate is from Latin *de, down*, 'completely' and *battere*, 'to fight, beat'.

Debenture is from Latin *debenture*, 'there are due'.

Debility comes from Latin *debilis*, 'weak', and has no connection with the word ability.

Debonair comes from Old French *de bonne aire* meaning 'of good disposition'.

Debris comes from French *de-* and *briser*, 'break'.

Debt is based on Latin *debere*, 'owe'.

A **debut** is a first public appearance; a **premiere** is a first performance, showing, or broadcast.

Decease actually means 'departure from life', from Latin *decessus*, 'departure'.

December was originally so named because it was the tenth month in the Roman calendar, derived from Latin *decem*, 'ten'.

Decibel is literally one-tenth of a bel, a unit of sound intensity.

Deciduous derives from Latin *deciduus*, 'falling down'.

Decimal is from Latin *decimus*, tenth from *decem*, 'ten'.

Decimate means 'to destroy in part', not entirely; the literal and original sense of decimate was 'put to death one person in ten'.

Decipher can also be spelled *decypher* and it first meant 'discover, find out;' a synonym is decrypt.

Declivity is a fancy name for a downward slope.

Decorate suggests relieving plainness or monotony by adding beauty through colour or design.

Decrease literally means 'ungrow' (Latin *decrescere*).

Decry is literally to 'cry down', i.e. 'denounce, condemn'.

Decumbiture is the act of going to bed when sick.

Deduce first meant 'to lead' (from Latin *ducere*, 'to lead').

Defatigable is apt to or capable of being wearied.

Defenestration is the act of throwing someone out the window (French *fenestra*, 'window').

Defer is from Latin *differre*, 'to carry apart, delay'.

Defervescence is a cooling down.

Defile is an alteration of defoul, 'to trample down, to tread on'.

Define comes from *de-* 'completely, thoroughly' and *finire*, 'finish', and firt meant 'bring to an end, settle'—hence, **definite**.

Defuse means to remove a fux—usually from an explosure.

Defy first meant renounce faith.

Deglutition is the act of swallowing.

Degressive means 'reducing by gradual amounts'.

Deity comes from Latin *dues*, 'god'

To take an oath is to **dejerate**.

A late breakfast can be called a **dejeuner**.

Deke is a shortened form of decoy.

Deleterious is based on a Greek word for 'noxious'.

Deletitious means pertaining to erasing.

Delibation is a taste or sip.

Delicious is the underlying meaning of 'tempting, luring from the straight and narrow', from Latin *delicia*, 'delight'.

Delight is from French *delitier*, from Latin *delectare*, 'to charm' and the change in spelling to '*gh*' was patterned on words like 'light'.

Deliver comes from latin *de-*, 'away' and *liberare*, 'liberate, set free'.

A **dell** is a small, secluded valley.

Deltiology is collecting or studying postcards.

Deluxe, once two words, is French for 'of luxury'.

Demeanour comes from the obsolete verb *demean*, 'behave'.

The **denominator** in a fraction is the part below the horizontal line (called the **separatrix**) and the **numerator** is above the line.

Demolish come from Latin *de-* and *moliri*, 'construct'.

The reading of tree rings for dating purposes is **dendrochronology**.

Dentiscalp is a fancy word for toothpick.

Dewlap is the loose fold of skin below the throat in cattle, dogs, etc.

Dine and **dinner** come from French *denser*, from *desjeuner*, 'to break a fast'; in Middle English **dinner** meant 'breakfast' or 'first big meal of the day'.

Dinful means noisy.

Dispense is ultimately from Latin *dispendere*, 'weigh out'.

Display first meant 'to unfold', coming from Latin *dis* and *plicare*, 'fold'.

Disrupt first meant 'break apart, separate forcibly'.

To **dissect** language is to parse it—as analysing the structure of a sentence.

Dissemble means to conceal, to give a false appearance; **disassemble** means to take apart.

Dissertation is from Latin *literally*, 'continue to discuss'; to **dissert** is to discuss or examine.

Distort first meant 'twist to one side'.

Distrait means 'absent-minded as a result of apprehension, worry, etc.' while. **Distraught** means 'agitated' and 'bewildered, distracted'.

To **distrust** is to suspect someone is dishonest; to **mistrust** is to merely lack confidence in someone.

Dictionary means 'under rule or dominion; subject', and the noun means 'subject; one who is under rule'.

Ditto is from Italian *ditto*, 'said aforesaid, spoken', and is abbreviated do, or expressed by two dots or commas or a dash.

A **dittology** is a double reading or interpretation.

Disturb is based on Latin *turba*, 'tumult', and **disturb** applies better to physical agitation and **perturb** to mental agitation.

A **dividend** can be a portion or share of anything divided.

DNA is the prime constituent of chromosomes and it controls the hereditary characterstics and synthesis of proteins within the cells of virtually all living beings; **RNA** is a complex mucleic acid in cells, that is involved in the synthesis of protien.

To **doattee** is to nod the head when sleep comes on while one is sitting.

Doctor in Latin means 'teacher'.

Docity is the ability to learn quickly.

Document first meant 'instruction' or 'evidence', whether written or not.

Dogfall is a draw or tie.

Doggerel is loosely styled verse with an irregular rhythm, usually intended to be comical.

An orphaned calf is a **dogie**.

Dogma is Greek for 'opinion'—but now it means principle(s) laid down as incontrovertible.

Dolor is mental pain or suffering, but it first meant physical pain.

Something that relieves or drives away sadness is **dolorifuge**.

A **domestic** animal is a pet a **domesticated** animal is a formerly wild animal bred for human use.

Domino was once slang for the teeth and also for the keys of a piano.

Doppelganger is borrowed from a German word meaning 'double-goer'.

Do-si-do is an alteration of French *dos-a-dos*, 'back-to-back'.

Dossier comes from French denoting a bundle of papers in a wrapper with a label on the back (from *dos*, 'back' based on Latin *dorsum*).

E

An abrupt tide rise is an **eagre**.

A mug's handle is the **ear**.

A small box of information at the top of a newspaper's front page is an **ear**.

Early is based on *ere*, 'before'.

Earnest was first a noun meaning 'seriousness of feeling'.

Earth the planet, is capitalized, while **earthenware**, low-fired clay, is not. **Porcelain** is high-fired, **stoneware** is about halfway between **earthenware** and **porcelain** in quality and durability, and the terms **china** can be applied to any **porcelain, earthenware** or ceramic ware dishes or crockery.

Eatertainment is dining combined with entertainment.

Ebriety is another word for drunkenness.

Ebullition is a sudden outburst of emotion or violence.

Ecceity is 'the quality of being present'.

Éclair is French for lightning bolt—perhaps for the speed with which one is eaten.

Ecology comes from Greek *okologie*, from *oikos*, 'home, habital' and *ology*.

Economic means 'pertaining to the production and use of income' and **economical** is 'avoiding waste, being careful of resources'.

Eczema is from Greek *ekzema*, 'eruption'.

Edacious means pertaining to eating. **Edacity** is a voracious appetite.

Edentate means 'without teeth'.

Edit first meant 'give it out, put out, publish'; **edit** as in 'prepare for publication' is a shortened form of 'editor'.

Editor is Latin word meaning literally 'producer (of games), publisher' from *edere*, 'to put out, produce'.

Effort first meant power and it comes from Latin *ef* and *fortis*, 'strong'.

Effrontery is from Latin *effroms*, 'barefaced, shameless'.

Effulgent means 'shining brilliantly'.

An **eft** is a small lizard or lizard-like animal, like a *newt*.

An **egeria** is a female advisor.

Eggplant was so named because the delicate white varieties resemble eggs.

Eisegesis is the interpretation of a word or passage by reading into it one's own ideas.

Either is the descendant of an ancient Germanic phrase meaning 'always each of two'.

Elbow-lifting is an euphemism for a fondness for drinking.

Eldorado means 'the gilded one'.

Election came via French from Latin *electionem*, from the earlier *eligere*, 'to choose, pick out'.

Electron is actually a combination of electric and on.

Elevate from Latin *elevare*, 'to raise', is based on *levis*, 'light'.

Elicit comes from a Latin stem meaning, 'draw forth by magic or trickery'.

Eligible means fit or entitled to be chosen and comes from Latin *eligere,* 'choose'.

Elude comes from *e,* 'out, away from' and *ludere,* 'to play'.

Elusion is the action of deluding someone—or an escape or evasion.

Emacity is an urge to buy.

Embolalia are useless or hesitation words or utterances in speech like 'oh, uh, you know, I mean'.

Embonpoint means plumpness, though in French *en bon point* means 'in good shape'.

Embrace's source is Latin *in* and *brachium,* 'arm' and the word implies a ready or happy acceptance.

Embryo comes from *em,* 'into' and *bruein,* 'swell, grow'.

Emerge is a combination of *e-* 'from' and Latin *merge,* 'to dip, plunge'.

Enthusiasm, from Greek *enthous,* first meant 'possessed or inspired by a god'.

Entomology the science of bugs/insects—is based on Greek *entomos,* 'insect'.

A light dish served between two courses of a formal meal or dishes served in addition to the main course of a meal is **entremets**.

Epalperbrate means 'without eyebrows'.

Epeolatry is the worship of words.

Epics are long poems about legendary heroes; **sagas** are prose epics about famous men and women especially of medieval times.

Epilogue is taken from Greek *epilogos,* from *epi,* 'in addition' and *logos,* 'speech'.

The **epimyth** is the moral of a story.

Epincian means 'celebrating victory'.

Epiphany was originally the appearance or manifestation of a divinity.

Episode, first a Greek dialogue between two songs, is from *eis,* 'into' and *hodos,* 'way'.

Epistaxis is a word for nosebleed.

Epistemology is the theory or science of the methods or grounds of knowledge.

Epistle is from Greek *epistole,* 'something sent to someone'.

Epistolary means 'of the nature of letters, contained in letters'.
Epitaph is from Greek *epi*, 'upon, over' and *taphos*, 'tomb' or 'funeral'.
A poem written to celebrate a wedding is an **epithalamium**.
An **epopt** is an overseer, watcher, or beholder.
An **epulation** is a feast.
Equator comes from Latin *aequator*, 'in full', *circulus aequator diet et noctis*, 'circle equalizing day and night'.
Equestrian comes from Latin *eques*, 'horseman', from *equus*, 'horse'.
An **era** is a system of numbering years from an important event.
Erenow means 'before this time'.
An **ergophile** is a person who loves to work.
A two-year-old canary is an **eriff**.
On **ewer** was a wide mouthed water jug formerly used in bedrooms.
Exact was first a verb, from Latin *ex*, 'thoroughly' and *agere*, 'perform'.
Exaggerate once meant 'accumulate, pile up'.
Exalt means to elevate, praise, or raise a person or thing; **exult** means to rejoice greatly.
An **exaltation** is a group of larks in flight.
An **examen** is a critical study.
Except is from Latin *ex*, 'out of' and *capere* 'take'.
Excerpt derives from Latin *ex-* 'out of' and *carpere*, 'to pluck'.
Exchange comes from Latin *cambire*, 'barter'.
Excruciating's root sense is 'to crucify'.
Excuse is from Latin *ex-* 'out', and *causa*, 'cause blame, accusation'.
An **exeat** is a leave of absence.
Execute derives from Latin *exsequi*, 'carry out, follow up punish'.
Executive first meant 'pertaining to execution, putting something into effect'.
An **exegesis** is an analysis of a word.
Exemplify can mean 'make an official copy of a document'.
Exfodiate means to dig out.
Exhume is from Latin *ex-*, 'out of' and *humus*, 'ground'.
Exigency is anything needed, demanded, or required.

Expand comes from Latin *ex-*, 'out' and *pandere*, 'to spread'.

Expedient means 'convenient in the circumstances' and suggests unfairness or dishonesty.

Expedite comes from a Latin word (literally 'free the feet') meaning 'put in order by freeing from difficulties'.

Expedition retains the notions of speed and purpose.

Expenditure refers to an actual outlay of money or goods, whereas *expense* has a more general sense, a charge or cost of goods or property. We have expenses, but we make expenditures.

Experience and **experiment** and **expert** derive from Latin *experiri*, 'try'.

Experrection is waking up or awakening.

To **expiate** is to make amends or reparation for.

Exponent as an adjective means 'expounding, interpreting'.

Extempore was literally 'out of the time' in Latin.

A synonym for astonishing is **extonious**.

Extort and extortion are from Latin *ex-*, 'out' and *torquere*, 'to twist'.

Extra is probably a shortening of extraordinary.

Extreme and **extremity** are from Latin *exter*, 'outer'.

Exult is from Latin *ex-*, 'out, upward' and *salire*, 'to leap'.

F

A **fainéant** is a person who does nothing, an idler.

Faint in 'faint of heart' means 'lacking in courage'.

Faith's root is Latin *fides* from *fidere*, 'trust'.

Faitour is a cheat or imposter.

Fan, as in enthusiast, is an abbreviation of fanatic, from Greek *phanatikos*, 'person from the temple'—a god-intoxicated person.

Fanatic comes from a Latin word for 'pertaining to a temple' or inspired by or frenzied by a god.

A **fanlight** is a semicircular or rectangular window over a door or other window.
Farewell is literally, 'go well'.
Far-fetched originally meant 'brought from far'.
A **farl** is a chunk of bread.
To **fastigate** is to make pointed .
Fastigiated means 'sloping up to a point'.
Fastuous means haughty, pretentious.
Fatal first meant 'decreed by fate'.
Fatstock is livestock fattened for slaughter.
Fatuous is derived from Latin *fatuus*, 'foolish'.
Faucet probably come from French meaning 'bore, tap'.
Faust is an adjective meaning happy.
Fear first meant 'sudden calamity' or 'danger'.
Someone may be **fearful**; someone or something may be **fearsome**.
Feasible means capable of being done (not probable or plausible).
Featous means well-proportioned or handsome.
February was the month of the festival of purification for the ancient Romans, '*Februa*', from Latin *februum*, 'purgation'.
To **feek** is to wander aimlessly.
To **feer** is to mark off land for plowing.
Fellowfeel is to share the feelings of others, sympathise with.
Female is a diminutive of *femina*, while male comes from latin *masculus*.
Fenugreek literally means 'Greek hay' as the Romans used this dried plant for fodder.
Feracious means fruitful, prolific.
Festival was for some time an adjective referring to a fest day of the church.
A **flexitarian** is one who is vegetarian at home but who will eat meat or fish in a restaurant or as a guest.
One meaning of **flight** is state of agitation or trembling.
Flinch used to mean 'slink, sneak off'.

Flippant once meant flexible, nimble, pliant.

A limb adapted for swimming is a **flipper**—like that of a penguin, seal, or turtle.

Flirt is either imitative of flick or spurt or both words.

To **flob** is to move clumsily or aimlessly.

Flonker is anything very large or outrageous.

Floor goes back to Proto-Germanic *floruz*, 'flat surface'.

The earliest sense of **floozy** (late 19c–early 20c) is 'a girl or young woman' and evolved quickly to one of questionable character.

Florescent refers to a time of blossoming or flowering.

Floss is a word for untwisted filaments of silk used in making embroidery or satin.

A **flummery** is an empty compliment.

A **flump** is a heavy sound of something moving, falling, or dropping heavily.

A **flurch** is a multitude or great many things (not persons).

To **flurn** is to show contempt by looks.

Flurry may be a blend of flutter and hurry.

Flush may be a blend of flash and gush. If something is aligned with a margin, it is **flush**.

Fluster first meant 'make slightly drunk'. Fluster and frustrate makes **flustrate**.

Fogdom is a region where nothing is clear, the state of fog.

Folio originally designated the largest size of book.

Format originally pertained to the physical characterstics of a book or other object—especially the shape or size.

Formication is a sensation of ants creeping over one's skin.

Formulate can mean 'reduce to a formula'.

Fortunate means good fortune, while **fortuitous** means merely happening by chance or accident.

A **fosse** is a canal, ditch, or trench and a fossette is a small hollow or depression (as in bone or stell).

Frown is from French *froigne*, 'surly look'—ultimately of Celtic origin.

Fructose (fruit sugar) is in green plants, fruits, and honey; **glucose**

is a simple sugar (also **dextrose**) is a simple sugar in grapes, corn, etc.

Fructuous means producing a great deal of fruit.

Fubbery is another word for cheating or deception.

Fulfil originally mean fill full, fill up.

Fulgent means 'dazzlingly bright'.

Fulvous means 'dull brownish yellow'.

Fume comes from Old French *fum*, from Latin *fumus*, 'smoke, steam'.

Fund's original and literal meaning is 'bottom' (Latin *fundus*) but changed to 'basic supply, as of money'.

Fungology is the science of fungi.

Funicular is literally 'running on a rope'.

Fundamentalism is now employed to refer to any person or group that is characterized as unbending, rigorous, intolerant, and militant.

Further suggests a removing of obstacles in the way of a desired advance.

Fuzz and **fuzzy** come from German *fussig*, 'spongy'.

To **fuzzle** is to intoxicate or confuse.

G

Gaffe is actually French for 'blunder'.

Gag was originally an ad-lib joke thrown in by an actor to throw another actor off his lines.

Gaga in French and originally meant 'senile person'.

Comedians are **gagsters**.

A big milk drinker is a **galactophagist**; babies are **galactophagous**.

Galaxy is from Greek *gala*, *galaktos*, 'milk' as in Milky Way and galaxy actually means 'circle of milk'.

The kitchen of a boat, aircraft, or camper is the **galley**.

A man of courage and spirit can be called a **galliard**.

Gallivant may come from French *gallant*, 'ladies' man' (from *galer*, 'to revel') and *avant*, 'forward'.

Galoot first had a nautical use, 'an inexperienced marine'.

Gherkin is from Dutch *gurkkijn*, a diminutive of *gurk*, 'cucumber' and it is an immature or small cucumber.

GI is an abbreviation of Government Issue.

Gift first meant 'bride price' and was borrowed from Old Norse.

Gignate means to originate or produce.

Ginger, the spice, gives us the figurative use of 'mettle' or 'spirit'.

A **gink** is a person of no consequence.

Gizzard is based on Latin *gigeria*, 'cooked entrails of fowl' and it is the strong muscular second stomach of birds in which food is finely ground.

The flat area of the forehead is the **glabella.**

Glacier comes from Latin *glacies*, ' ice'; a **glacialist** studies ice and its impact on geology.

Glam is a word for the loud noise of talking or merrymaking.

Glamour first meant 'magic, enchantment' or 'art of contriving magic spells'.

Glaucoma comes from a Greek word meaning 'bluish green or grey' from a type of colour haze affecting the eyes; the word was formerly used to denote cataracts.

A person who cuts and fits glass is a **glazier.**

Gleet is sticky, slimy, or greasy filth.

To **gloat** once had the meaning to gaze, stare or to glow (Danish *gloe*).

Glob may be a blend of blob and gob.

Globe, from Latin *globus*, is related to *gleba*, 'lump of earth' and etymologically was 'something rolled up into a ball'.

To be **gloppened** is to be surprised.

A **glory** is a circle of light around the head of a saint or Jesus.

A **glout** is a frown or sullen look.

Glox is the sound of liquid when shaken in a barrel.

Greek *glukus*, 'sweet' is the ancestor of **glucose**, the variant *glukeros* was used by a chemist to coin *glycerin/glycerine* for 'syrupy liquid'.

To **gnap** means to criticise.

Gnathonic means 'sycophantic, parasitic'.

A **gnomology** is a collection of maxims, sayings, or precepts.

Goat may etymologically be 'animal that jumps about'.

Goblocks are large mouthfuls.

Go-cart first meant 'baby walker' as go has an obsolete sense 'walk'.

Goodish means moderately good.

Goof may have come from the earlier *goff*, an obsolete word meaning 'stupid person'.

A **grocer** (literally, 'dealer in gross') was originally a wholesale dealer and someone who sold the food in retail amounts was called a 'spicer' — so a wholesale dealer in these goods was called a 'spicer en gross' or 'grosser' (from French *gros*, 'great, large').

A **grocery** store is smaller; **a supermarket** is big.

Grog was part of a nickname of a Royal Navy admiral who ordered rum rations watered down to curb drunkenness; the nickname came from his coat's material, 'grogram' (from French *gros*, 'grain').

Grapple means 'to grope' or 'to come to grips with'.

To **grouk** is to become gradually enlivened after waking.

Groundsel may etymologically mean 'ground-swallower'.

Grub first referred to root vegetables which had to be grubbed (dug) out of the ground.

Gruesome is from an earlier verb grue, 'be terrified'.

Guard first meant 'care, keeping'.

Gubernation is the act of controlling or governing.

Gubernatorial and **governor** trace back to Latin *gubernare*, 'to govern' but governor took a detour through French (*governeor*).

Guerrilla is from a Spanish diminutive of *Guerra* war and refers to a soldier of an independent armed resistance force.

Gorilla is the ape.

Gulf comes from Greek *kolphos*, 'bosom'.

Gullet is from Latin *gula*, throat.
Gunny, the material used for sacks, is made from jute (from Sanskrit *gani*, 'sack').
To **guttle** is to eat gluttonously, voracioulsy .
Guttural is from Latin *guttur*, 'throat'.
Gymnasium was a school where Greek youths were given athletic training while naked (*gymnos*).
Gynecology is from the Greek word for 'woman', *gune*.

H

Hangout originally meant a place of business—from the signs 'hung out' by artisans, professionals, and tradespeople.
Hanky-panky may be an alteration of hokey-pokey.
Haphazard is redundant, with both components meaning 'chance'.
Hapless means one is lacking hap 'good fortune, luck'; the words happy and happiness also have the root 'hap'.
Haptic means pertaining to the sense of touch.
Hardiment is a word for boldness, courage, or daring.
Harm's original meaning was 'grief' before 'physical damage'.
A **hasp** is a piece of hardware used to lock a door or gate; it fits over a staple or loop and padlock through that secures the door or gate.
A **harridan** is an ill-tempered, scolding woman.
Hassle may be a blend of haggle and tussle.
Hate means to 'dislike intensely, loathe' and **despise** means 'look down on contemptuously'.
Haul originally had the nautical meaning of 'to trim the sails to sail closer to the wind'.
Hazard started as the name of a game of dice but later extended to all kinds of risks and comes from Arabic *az-zohr*, 'gaming dice'.
Haze is probably a back-formation from hazy.
HAZMAT stands for Hazardous Material.
He ultimately comes from Indo-European *ki-/ko-*, 'this, here'—as

opposed to 'that, there'.

A ship's bathroom is the **head**.

Hearse was once the decorative bier, frame, or stand on which a corpse was laid, or a framework to carry candles over a coffin.

Heartburn has on old meaning of 'jealousy' or 'hatred'.

The **hearth** is the floor of a fireplace and the area in front of a fireplace.

The **dent** at the end of your sternum is the **heart-spoon**.

Hebephrenic describes the condition of adolescent silliness.

Hectic was originally a medical term for a type of fever.

Heirloom is a combination of heir and loom 'tool, utensil' and it describes any personal property that has been in a family for several generations.

Helicopter comes from Greek *helika*, 'screw' and *pteron*, 'wing'.

'**Hello**,' which was on exclamation of surprise dating back to the Middle Ages, from French *hallow*, 'to pursue by shouting,' first becoming 'hallo' in English.

Hepatic (pertaining to or affecting the liver) is from Greek *hepatikos*, 'of the liver,' and **Hepatitis** is *hepatos*, 'liver' and *-itis*, 'inflammation'.

Latin *heres*, '**heir**' gives us **hereditary**, **heir**, **heritage**, and more.

Horoscope comes from Greek *hora*, 'hour, time' and *skopos*, 'observer'.

Horripilating is getting goosebumps from the cold.

Horseplay originally was a play in which a horse was used or took part—or theatrical horsemanship.

Hotchpotch/hodgepodge is an alteration of the earlier hotchpot, borrowed from Old French *Hocher*, 'shake' and *pot*, 'pot' ('shake the pot').

HOV stands for high-occupancy vehicle.

A conical building enclosing a kiln is a **hovel**.

Howdy is a shortened form of 'How do you do?'.

Hub first meant 'a shelf at the side of a fireplace used for heating pans'.

Hubris is Greek, literally 'insolence'.

Hue and cry is somewhat redundant as **hue** means 'shout, make an outery'; **hue** and **cry** was a medieval law requiring that all citizens within earshot give chase to a fleeing criminal.

Hug is probably of Scandinavian origin—tracing to words meaning 'comfort, console' and 'affection'.

Humiliate is from Latin *humilis*, 'humble'.

Hummacky means 'having an uneven surface'.

Hurdle refers to a difficulty or obstacle; **hurtle** means to move with great speed and violence.

Hurly-burly is turmoil or an uproar.

Hurrah, hurray, and **hooray** are alterations *of* **huzza**, a sailor's cheer.

Husband comes from the German words *hus* and *bundo*, meaning 'houseowner' and originally had nothing to do with marital status; in Old English, **husband** was literally 'housebound'—bound to the house and family.

The word **hussy** is just a corruption of 'housewife' and originally had no unkind implications and for many years was not applied to a married woman.

Hydraulic comes from Greek *hydro*, 'water' and *aulos*, 'pipe'.

Hydroponics comes from combining *hydro-* with *ponos*, 'labour' and is patterned on geoponics; **hydroponics** is also known as aquaculture or tank farming.

A **hydropot** is a water drinker and a **galactophagist** is a milk drinker.

A **hyperdisyllable** is a word of more than two syllables.

Difficulty in making decisions is **hypobulia**.

Hyponoia is hidden meaning or significance.

A vague feeling of sadness, seemingly without cause is **hypophrenia** and a vague feeling of mental discomfort is **malnoia**.

Hyposomnia is another way of saying lack of sleep.

Profound melancholy can be called **hypothimia**.

I

Idem is the Latin word for ditto.

Another name for a trademark is an **idiograph**.

Ignore is properly used of things that are present in our surroundings; but for things like rules, conventions, stipulations, contracts, the right word is **disregard**.

Ignore and **ignorant** are from Latin *i-*, 'not' and *gno-*, 'know'.

Impresario comes from the Italian word *impresa*, 'undertaking'.

Impress stresses the depth and persistence of the effect.

An **imprest** is a monetary advance, from the obsolete verb **imprest** 'to lend'.

To **imprint** is to cause a young animal to accept its parent as the proper object of affection; the learning process of young animals is called **imprinting**.

Impromptu is based on Latin *in promptu*, 'in readiness' from *promptus*, 'prepared, ready'.

Improve first meant 'to make a profit for oneself' or 'to employ to advantage; to make profitable use of'.

Inane, from Latin *inonis*, first meant 'empty', words meaning 'babbling, full of idle talk'; include **inaniloquent** and **inaniloquous**.

Inapt is 'not suitable or appropriate' while **unapt** is 'not likely or inclined'.

Inaugurate is from Latin *inauguruat-*, 'interpreted as omens (from the flight of birds)', from *augurare*, 'to auger'.

Incense once meant to kindle any passion, good or bad.

Inch-meal means gradually or by inches or small degrees.

The base of **incinerate** is Latin *ciner-*, 'ashes'; an **incipient** is a beginner.

Incognito is Italian 'unknown, disguised,' from Latin *incognitus*, 'unknown'.

Income originally meant 'arrival, entrance'; a place of entrance can be called an **incoming**.

Incredible means 'unbelievable' and **incredulous** means 'unbelieving'.

Indagatrix is a female searcher or investigator.

Induce can mean 'derive by reasoning from facts'; the base of **induce** and **induction** is Latin *ducere*, 'to lead'.

ISBN stands for International Standard Book Number and each book has a unique one.
Islamania is a passion for islands.
Words that don't repeat any letters are known as **isograms**.
Isometric is from Latin *isus*, 'equal' and *metria*, 'measuring'.
Issue and **exit** are closely related, going back to Latin *exire*, 'go out,' which became Old French *eissue* and later **issue**, and Latin *exitus* and then exit.
Isuzu means '50 bells' in Japanese.
The name of the letter Z is **izzard**.

J

Jacent means 'lying, recumbent'—so **adjacent** means 'lying next to'.
A **jackleg** is a reckless driver.
Jaded originally referred to a 'worn-out' horse.
January is named for Janus, the Roman god of gates and doors and beginnings, who had two faces—one looking forward to the future and one looking backward to the past.
Jargogle means 'to confuse, to mix up'.
The original sense of **jargon** was 'chattering, twittering,' and then 'gibberish'—coming from French *jargoun*, 'warbling of birds'.
Jaundice is based on French *jaune*, 'yellow'.
Jazz can mean 'energy, excitement'.
A **jazzbo** is a jazz musician.
Jeans are made of cloth that was originally called Gene fustian or Geane, the name for Genoa, Italy, in Middle English; **jeannette** is any fabric resembling jean.
Jest first meant 'exploit, heroic deed' and then 'a story of heroic deeds'—from Latin *gesta*, 'exploito, actions'.
Jesus means 'anointed one' and Buddha means 'the Enlightened'.

Jewel may be from French *Jeu*, 'play,' and some say from Latin *jocus*, 'jest'.

Jiffy is an actual unit of time—1/60 or 1/50 of a second.

A **jilt** is a woman accomplice to a thief.

The gold circles on a tambourine's edge are the **jingles**.

Joinhand is an old name for cursive writing.

A **joist** is a parallel timber to which floor boards or ceiling laths are fastened. Latin *locus*, 'jest, **joke**' gave us **joke**.

Jolly comes from Old French *jolif*, 'merry, festive, pleasant'.

Journey's first sense was a day's (*jour*) travel.

Judge is from Latin *jus*, 'law,' and *dicere*, 'to say'.

Judicial means 'pertaining to judges or the courts' and **judicious** means 'prudent, carefully considered'; **judicial** refers to judgement as it is exercised by the court, **judicious** to judgement as exercised by an individual.

Juggle is from Latin *joculus*, a diminutive of *jocus*, 'jest,' and a **juggler** was originally a jester.

July and **August** were originally named, respectively, Quintilis (fifth) and Sextilis (sixth) month; September is *septem*, 'seven,' November *novem*, 'nine,' and December *decem*, 'ten'; both **July** and **August** are named for Roman Empire leaders: Julius Caesar and Augustus Caesar.

Jumbo originally denoted a large and clumsy person and the word may come from Swahili *jambe*, 'chief'.

June is either named for Juno, the queen of the Roman gods and the goddess of marriage—or named for Junius, a prominent ancient Roman family.

The art of taking photographs of people jumping, in order to capture their essence and also for scientific study, is **jumpology**.

Juventude is another word for 'youth'.

K

Kalon is the kind of beauty that is more than skin deep.
Kaput was originally a card game term for 'being without tricks' in the game piquet.
Karaoke means 'empty orchestra' in Japanese.
Karoshi is death caused by overwork.
Kedogenous is 'brought about by worry or anxiety'.
Keister first meant 'suitcase' or 'satchel'.
To **kelk** is to groan or belch.
Kempt means 'combed' or 'neatly kept'.
Kerosene is based on Greek *keros*, 'wax'.
Khaki comes from Persian *khak*, 'dust, earth'.
Kid originally denoted a young goat.
Kindergarten is German for 'children's garden'—a term for a school in which children's aptitude for learning is cultivated.
A **kine** is an isolated body movement or gesture.
Kinemics is the study of gestures as units of expression.
Kinesics and **pasimology** are other terms for body language.
Kitty (now pool of money) may be from the slang meaning of 'jail'.
Knabble means to bite or nibble.
Knickknack has two k's in the middle.
Know is from an Indo-European root shared by Latin (*g*)*noscere* and Greek *gignoskein*.
Knowledge is the information held on a computer system; the word was originally a verb meaning 'acknowledge, recognize'.
Kowtow comes from Chinese *kou tou*, 'knock one's head' which would occur during prostration out of respect, worship, etc.
Kudos is best pronounced KYOO-dahs or KYOO-dohs and derives from Greek *kydos*, 'glory, praise, renown'; in Greek, it means a single bit of praise or prestige, but the word looks like an English plural and is therefore treated as one.
A **kyle** is a narrow sea channel between two islands (from Scottish).

L

Labefaction is a deterioration or downfall.

Label, originally meaning 'narrow band or strip', comes from a French word meaning 'ribbon'.

The word for 'the ability to read lips' is **labiomancy**.

Lackadaisical comes from an old term **lackadoy**, which means 'Shame on you, dayl' as if it were a person.

Laclabphily is said to be the collecting of cheese labels.

Lad meant 'servant' before it acquired a more general sense of 'youth'.

Lady is from Old English *hlaf*, 'loaf' and a Germanic base meaning 'knead' and first literally meant 'one who kneads bread'.

Lair first meant 'grave, tomb' or 'place where one sleeps'.

Lake first meant pool or pond.

Landscape comes from Dutch *landschap*, 'region, tract of land'.

Language is from Latin *lingua*.

Languor is any distressed condition, such as illness, sorrow, fatigue, etc.

Lapidary first meant 'pertaining to stones'.

To **lapidate** is to pelt someone with stones.

Lappet is a fold or hanging piece of flesh in some animals.

Larceny comes from *larcin*, the French word for mercenary soldier — as they were expected to indulge in petty theft.

Lascivious means 'inclined to lust'.

Laser is an acronym for Light Amplification by Stimulated Emission of Radiation.

Lassitude is mental weariness.

Late comes from Indo-European *lad-*, 'slow, weary' which begat Latin *lassus*, 'tired' before English late, 'slow'.

Latent means 'hidden, concealed' and its opposite is patent.

Latescent means 'becoming obscure or hidden away'.

A **laud** is a hymn of praise.

Laudable means deserving praise; **laudatory** means expressing praise.

Laundry comes from Latin *lavare*, 'wash'—as does lavatory, which first meant 'place or vessel for washing'.

Lavender got its name from the custom of adding it to the laundry and baths (Latin *lavare*, 'to wash'); lavender once meant 'laundress'.

Lavish traces back to French *lavache*, 'deluge of rain'.

Lawn comes from laund, 'a glade or pasture'.

A **layette** is a set of clothing, accessories, and equipment for a new baby.

One meaning of **leave** is 'approval, pleasure'.

A **lectern** is the stand on which the speaker's notes are placed, the **podium** is the platform on which the speaker and **lectern** stand, a **platform** for several people is a **dais**, and a **rostrum** is a platform for one or more.

The finger next to the little finger is the **leech-finger**.

Leek is from German and forms the second syllable of garlic.

Leg-of-mutton sleeves means that they resemble a leg of mutton, very full and loose on the arm but close-fitting at the wrist.

Lens is from Latin for '*lentil*' because of the similarity in shape.

Lesson etymologically, is 'something read,' from Latin *lectio*, 'reading', from *legere*, 'read'—so lesson is literally the action of reading to oneself.

Lethonomia is the inability to recall the right name.

Letter is from Latin *littera*, 'alphabetic symbol' or, in the plural, 'document'.

Leukemia is from Greek *leukas*, 'white' and *emia* (from *haima*) 'blood'.

Leviathan is Hebrew for a sea monster which can only be subdued by God, so it came to mean a very large or powerful thing.

Level is base on latin *labella*, diminutive of *librs*, 'balance, scales'.

Lexicography is the art of defining words or compiling lexicons.

A dictionary and wordbook collector is a **lexiconophilist**.

Libberwort is food or drink that makes one idle and stupid, food of no nutritional value, i.e., junk food.

Libertine first meant freedman or son of a freedman.

Licit means not forbidden by law; allowable the opposite or illicit.

Lieu instead is from Middle English via French from Latin *locus*, 'place'.
Lightsome can mean not weighed down by cares.
Light-time is the time required for light to travel from a distant object to Earth.
Lilt comes from a word meaning pipe and the noun originally meant 'song, tune'.
Limaceous means slug-like or pertaining to slugs.
Logology is the pursuit of word puzzles; also the science or words.
Loiter may come from Middle Dutch *loteren*, 'wag about'.
Longevity is from Latin *longus*, 'long', and *aevum*, 'age', literally 'long life'.
Loo is probably a fanciful form of French *l'eau*, 'the water'.
Lorate means shaped like a strap.
A **lorimer** is a saddle-maker.
To **lout** is to treat with contempt.
Louvre comes from French *lovier*, 'skylight' and was first a domed turret-like part of a roof for smoke to leave or light to come in.
Love in tennis comes from *l'oeuf*, 'egg' as a zero looks like an egg; we sometimes call zero a 'goose egg'.
Lubricous means slippery (literally or figuratively).
Lugubrious means mournful; sorrowful payment of ransom is **luition**.
Lunacy is insanity, once believed to be brought on by changes in the moon.
Lunatic can mean influenced by the moon.
Lunch comes from Scottish *lonch*, a 'hunk of meat' and it first meant hunk, thick piece, a large piece of anything, especially edible like bread or cheese.
Luscious may be an alteration of obsolete **licious**, a shortened form of delicious.
Lusk means lazy or sluggish.
Lusory is used as a pastime or playful.

Lutose means covered with mud.
Lycanthropy is a type of insanity in which the patient imagines himself a beast.

M

Macrology is long and tiresome talk.
Madam is French, literally, 'my lady'.
Market is from Old Provencal *mercari*, 'by', and the word originally denoted 'a place where people met to trade goods' (from Latin *mercatus*); **mart** is a variant.
Marmalade comes from Portuguese *marmelada*, 'quince' jam, from Latin *melomeli*, 'honey flavoured with quinces', and *melimela*, sweet apple.
Mascara comes from an Italian word for mask.
Mascot is from Provencal *masco*, 'sorcerer', witch a person or thing that is supposed to bring good luck.
Massage probably comes from Arabic *massa*, 'to feel, handle, palpate'.
Master is from Latin *magister*, 'chief'.
Masticate is from Greek *mastikhan*, 'gnash' or 'grind the teeth'.
Mathematical is base on Greek, *mathema*, 'science', from *manthanein*, 'learn mathematic(s)' first referred to 'something learned'.
Matinee, literally French for morning, is so called because these performances once took place in the morning.
Matins is a morning church service or the first mass of the day.
Matriculation is formal admission to a college or university and is based on Latin *matricula*, 'register, catalog'.
Matrimony is from Latin *matrimonium*, 'state of being married', from *mater*, 'mother', and *monium, mony* ('state, condition').
Matter is from Latin *material*, 'timber' or 'stuff of which something is made or subject of discourse'.
Mattoid means semi-nuts or behaving erratically.

Mattress comes from Arabic al-*matrah*, 'bed, carpet, cushion, seat'.

Maudlin is a corruption of Magdalene, the woman who weeped at the feet of Jesus as he was crucified.

Maundy descends from a Latin word meaning commandment, so **Maundy** Thursday refers to the mandate given by Jesus at the Last Supper.

Mayor's ancestor is Latin *maior*, 'person in authority', from *maior*, 'greater'.

Meat first meant food, nourishment, especially solid food as opposed to drink.

A **meatus** is a channel or passage.

Mediocre is from Latin *mediocris*, of 'middle height' or degree, from Latin *medius, mid*, and *ocris*, 'rugged mountain'.

Mien is from Chinese for 'wheat flour' and these are wheat flour noodles used in dishes like lo mein, chow mein (note change of spelling).

If someone is in a **miff,** they are in a fit of pique or a huff.

Milieu is from Latin *medius*, 'mid', and *lieu*, 'place'.

Minaret derives from Turkish *minaret*, 'lighthouse, tall tower'.

Mindshare is the consumer awareness of a brand or product.

Minikin refers to a petite or dainty person.

Minimize means to reduce to an absolute minimum—not to play down or soften.

Minister was originally a person acting under the authority or as an agent of another.

Mint as in money comes from Latin *moneta*.

Minuscule comes from medieval manuscript writing, literally, *minscula littera*, 'somewhat smaller letter.'

A **misnancy** is an effeminate character.

A **misologist** is one who is averse to conflict, but a **misologist** may also be one who does not want to discuss something but prefers to plunge ahead.

A person who cannot stand learning is a **misomusist**.

Miss is a shortened form of mistress.

A **mittimus** is an official order sending someone to prison.

Mizle means to 'lead astray, to deceive'.

Mizmaze is confusion or bewilderment.

Fine or light rain or drizzle can be called **mizzle**.

Mnemotechnics is another name for memory techniques.

Mob is from Latin *mobile vulgus*, which meant 'the masses' or 'disorderly crowd'.

Modest comes from Latin *modestus*, 'keeping due measure'.

A napkin tucked in a collar to protect clothes is a **mokador** or **bib**.

Molest first meant to 'cause trouble' or 'annoy, vex'.

Money comes from *moneta*, a Latin word that was an epithet of the goddess Juno, in whose temple a mint was housed.

Latin **momentum**, from *movere*, 'move' and *mentum*, is the source of **moment**, which first meant moving power and is obviously the source of **momentum**.

Monday is 'day of the Moon', a translation of *lunas dies* (Latin).

N

Nadir (pronounced NAY-dur) is the point directly under your feet.

Name is ancient and goes back to Indo-European *nomen*, then Latin *nomen*, and Greek, *onoma*.

To **name-check** is to mention or acknowledge by name.

Napalm is the compound naphthemic palmitate.

The nasty-smelling mothball substance is **naphthalene**.

Narcotic is from Greek *narkoun*, 'make numb'.

A **natkin** is a disagreeable taste or smell.

Naupathia is seasickness.

Neat as in 'clean, clear' comes from Latin *nidus*, 'shining, clean'; **neat** first meant 'free from impurities'.

A **nebula** is a dust cloud in outer space.

Neck originally was just the back portion of the body connecting the head and shoulders.

Needle has the same Indo-European base as Latin *nere*, 'to spin,' and Greek *nema*, 'thread'.

Neighbour is Germanic *neigh/neah*, 'near', and *gebur*, 'dweller'.

Neoteny is the prolongation of the period of immaturity.

Nerve comes from Latin *nevus*, 'sinews, bowstring'.

Net as in 'without deductions' came from French *net* as 'neat' and then evolved to *net*, 'free from any (further) deduction'.

Netop is a synonym for friend.

News first meant 'new things, novelties'.

Niche is from Old French *ninchier*, 'make a nest'.

Nickname is from a misdivision of 'an eke-name' (*eke* meaning 'addition') into 'neke-name'.

Nifty is a name for a joke or witty remark.

Night-shine is a term for faint light perceptible at night.

Nikhedonia is the pleasure derived from anticipating success.

Ninny-broth was another name for coffee.

A **nip** is one-fourth of a bottle or a half-pint (of ale, especially), a **baby** is one-eighth of a bottle of wine.

Nitwit comes from Dutch *niet wit*, 'I don't know'.

A **nob** is a person of elegance and high social standing.

Noctidial means 'lasting for or comprising a night and a day'.

A **noddary** is a foolish act.

A **noggin** is another name for mug or cup.

To **noggle** is to walk awkwardly.

Noise first meant quarreling and comes from Latin *nausea*, 'feeling of disgust'.

N**oisome** means 'evil-smelling, offensive' and it comes from *noy*, a shortened form of annoy.

Nomad comes from the base of Greek *nemein*, 'to pasture'.

Nominate means call the name of (Latin *nomen*), while **denominate** means to give a name to.

Nonchalant comes from French *nonchaloir*, 'not heated', ultimately from Latin *noncalere*, 'not warm or aroused'.

Noology is the science of intuition and reason as phenomena of the mind.

Noon is derived from the Latin word for 'ninth' as it originally meant the ninth hour after sunrise, about 3 pm.

Neither **noon** nor **midnight** is 12 am or 12 pm because neither comes before or after the moment the sun is on the meridian.

Nor is a contraction of Old English *nother*, 'neither'.

The **nose-piece** is the part of eyeglasses that rest on the nose.

A **nosology** is a classification or list of diseases.

Nostalgia comes from Greek *nostos*, 'homeward journey, return home' and *algos*, 'pain' — the word *nostos* originally referring to the journey of Odysseus and the heroes from Troy.

Nostril comes from Old English words meaning 'nose hole'.

Notary is from Latin *notarlus*, 'shorthand writer or clerk'.

A **notelet** is a short note or notecard.

Notify first meant 'take note of, notice, observe'.

Nourish first meant 'bring up, or rear (a child or animal)'.

Nova was originally a new star or *nebula*.

Italian *novella storia*, 'new story' begat **novel**.

Noxious comes from Latin *noxius*, 'harmful'.

Nubile etymologically means 'suitable for marriage,' from Latin *nubere*, 'take a husband'.

Nucal means pertaining to nuts.

Number is regularly used with count nouns, while **amount** is mainly used with mass nouns: **number** of mistakes, **amount** of money.

Numeracy is having arithmetic skills (like literacy for reading).

Nuncheon was the first name for lunch, from *noon schenche* (drink) — a drink taken at noon.

Nyctalopia is poor vision in low light.

Nylon is an invented word patterned on 'cotton' and 'rayon'.

O

One who is **obdurate** is stubbornly impenitent.

Obese is from Latin *obesus*, literally 'having eaten oneself fat'.

Oblique can mean 'indirect,' as in a course or expression.

A meaning of **obliterate** is to cancel a postage stamp.

Oboxious first meant 'subject or liable to harm or injury' (Latin *ob-*, 'toward,' and *noxa*, 'harm, injury').

Obscene comes from Latin *obscenus*, 'ill-omened' or 'indecent'.

Obtain can mean 'prevail, succeed, win'.

The **occiput** is the back of the head (Latin *ob-*, and *caput*, 'head').

The **occident** is the region of the sky where the sun sets—the west (the opposite of **Orient**, the east).

Occult first meant 'hidden from sight; concealed' (Latin *ob-*, and *celare*, 'conceal').

Occupy's Latin root is *ob-*, 'over,' and *capere*, 'seize, take'.

Occur comes from Latin *occurrere*, 'run to meet'.

O'clock is an abbreviation for 'of the clock.'

The original meaning of **octave** was, 'eight-day festival'.

The Roman year originally began in March, so **October** (Latin *octo*, 'eight') was the eighth month.

Something's **odour** is its **reputation** or **estimation**.

Odoriferous means 'having an odour or fragrance' while **odorous** refers to something smelly.

An **oenologist** is a 'student of wine'.

Ogle which is 'to cast amorous glances' comes from Dutch *oog*, 'eye'.

Oikology is housekeeping.

Oil is from Latin *oleum* and that is from Greek *elaion*, 'olive **oil**; other oily substance'.

Olfactory comes from Latin *olere*, 'to smell,' and *facere*, 'make'.

Olitory means pertaining to or grown in a kitchen garden.

Ombrology is the study of rain.
Omphalophobia is a fear of belly buttons.
Oncology (study and treatment of tumours) is based on Greek *onco-*, 'mass'.
Oneiric means 'pertaining to dreams'.
Oneiromancy is dream interpretation.
Onion comes from the Latin word *unio*, 'oneness' (*unus*, 'one') as it consists of a single bulb.
On-line should generally be hyphenated as an adjective or adverb.
Onomatomania is a fear of a particular word.
Ontology is the branch of metaphysics concerned with the nature or essence of being or existence, the opposite of phenomenology (the science of phenomena).
Onymous means 'bearing the name of the author' (with the opposite being anonymous) or 'having a name'.
Opal comes from Sanskrit *upala*, 'precious stone'.
Opinion comes via Old French from Latin *opinari*, 'think'.
A cross between an orange and a tangerine is an **ortanique**.
Orthodontics, based on Greek *orthos*, 'straight,' is the branch of dentistry that aims to straighten crooked teeth.
Orthography is correct or proper spelling.
Orthology is the study of the correct use of words.
Orthopraxy is another way of saying 'right practice, right conduct' (**orthodoxy** is 'right belief, rightness of beliefs').
Ostrich is from Latin *avis struthio*, 'bird **ostrich**,' from Greek *strouthos*, '**ostrich** sparrow'.
Other is part of a large Germanic word family expressing 'alternative'.
Outstanding as a noun once meant projection.
Overkill first meant 'excessive killing'.
The upper lip is the **overlip**.
To **overlook** and to **overshadow** both meant 'to bewitch' at one time.
Overt first meant 'open, not closed'.
Owe first meant 'own, possess'.

Owl is from a Germanic base imitating the **owl's** call.

Oxymoron (guest host, jumbo shrimp) is from Greek *oxmoron*, a compound formed from *os*, 'sharp,' and *mors*, 'dull'.

An unusually shrill voice is **oxyphonic**.

Ozostomia is another word for bad breath.

P

Pacific and **pacify** trace back to Latin *pax*, 'peace'.

Paddock is from Old English *pearroc*, 'enclosure'.

A **paean** is a song of praise or thanksgiving or an expression of praise or admiration.

Pair is from Latin *par*, 'equal'.

Pakistan got its name from the initials of Punjab, Afghanistan, Kashmir plus the ending *-istan*, 'place, country'.

Pal comes from the gypsy word *prot* or *phral*, 'brother'.

Palinoia is the compulsive repetition of an act until it is perfect.

Panacea combines *pan-*, 'all,' and Greek *akos*, 'remedy'.

Etymologically, **pancreas** (the gland) means 'all flesh'.

A **panegyric** is a speech of praise, as a eulogy or encomium.

Panmnesia is the belief that every mental impression remains in the memory.

Pants comes from pantaloons—from a sixteenth century Italian comic called Pantalone who wore strange trousers.

Paparazzi (plural) got their name from paparazzo, a fictional freelance photographer in Fellini's 1959 film 'La Dolce Vita'; *paparazzo* in Italian means 'a buzzing insect'.

Paracentral is 'near the centre'.

The beginning of decline or decay is the **paracme**, the stage after one's peak.

Paraffin, coined from Latin *parum affinis*, '(having) little affinity'—

resists chemical combination.
Paralipophobia is a fear of having neglected some duty.
Paralysis is from a Greek word meaning 'disabled at the side'.
Paranoia is from Greek *para*, 'irregular,' and *noos*, 'mind'.
Passion first meant the suffering of pain and is from Latin *passionem*, 'suffering,' as used to describe the sufferings of Jesus Christ.
Parvanimity is 'meanness'.
Pashmina is derived from a Persian word meaning 'woollen'.
Pasta is literally 'dough' or 'paste' in Italian; **paste** first meant 'dough' or 'pastry'.
Pastime is derived from 'pass time'.
Pathetic first meant 'producing an effect on the emotions'.
A **pathic** is a passive person or victim.
Pathology literally means 'the study of suffering' but is actually used to describe the study of diseases.
Pathos (pronounced PAY-thos) is an English use of a Greek word for 'suffering'.
Patriarch is from Greek *patria*, 'family,' and *arkhes*, 'ruling'.
Pavement is from Latin *pavimentum*, 'trodden down or beaten floor'.
Pawn, the chess term, comes from Latin *pedo*, 'foot soldier' (from *pes*, 'foot').
Pea comes from Greek *pison*, 'pulse, pease'.
The small wooden ball inside a referee's whistle is called a **pea**.
Peak means 'maximize', **peek** means 'to peep or snoop', and **pique** means 'to excite or irritate'.
Peanut takes its name from its resemblance to peas in a pod and has these synonyms: pinda, goober, groundnut, ground pea, earthnut, and monkey nut.
The rough grainy feel of some paper is called **pebble**.
Peck can be slang for 'food'.
Pecorino cheese is from ewe's milk, as *pecora* is Italian for 'sheep'.
Cattle and sheep were an ancient medium of barter and exchange and the word **pecuniary** is from Latin *pecu*, 'cattle'.

Pediatrician, comes from Greek *pais/paidos*, 'child,' and *iatros*, 'physician'.
Pedigerous means 'having feet or legs'.
Peek first meant 'look through a crevice'.
Peeve is a back-formation from peevish 'perverse, obstinate'.
Pelican is probably based on a Greek word for *'ax'* — referring to the shape of its bill.
Pellucid means 'allowing the passage of light'.
Pen comes from Latin *penna*, 'feather'.
Pennant is a blend of pendant and pennon.
Pentecost means fiftieth day, as it occurs on the seventh Sunday after Easter.
People comes from Latin *populous*.
Pepper comes from Sanskrit *pippali*, 'long **pepper**'; **pep** is an abbreviation of **pepper**.
Pied means 'having two or more different colours' and first had the sense 'black and white like a magpie'.
Pillage is from French *piller*, 'plunder'.
A **pillowcase** can be called a **pilliver** or a **pillow—bere**.
Pilose means 'having soft hair'.
A small powerful spotlight is a **pinspot**.
A towing vehicle's rear hook or bolt is the **pintle**.
Pioneer was first used as military term for an infantryman (French *pionnier*, 'foot soldier').
Pious was probably borrowed from Lating *pius*, 'dutiful, kind'.
Pixel is a blend of pix (pics) and el(ement).
Pizza is literally 'pie' in Italian and pizze is a plural of **pizza**.
The material covering a zipper or fastener is called the **placket**.
A **plaint** is an audible protest.
Plaintiff once meant 'person who complains of illness'.
Planet comes from Greek *planets*, 'wanderer'.
Plaque comes from Dutch *plak*, 'tablet'.
Etymologically, a **plate** is something 'flat,' from Latin *plattus*, 'flat,'

and Greek *platys*, 'broad'.

Plateau can refer to an ornamented dish or tray for serving food.

A **plinth** is a squared base of a column, pedestal, piece of furniture, etc.

A **plongeur** is a dishwasher, busperson, or other menial worker in a restaurant or hotel.

Plot as in 'secret scheme' comes from Old French *complot*.

Pneumatic is etymologically 'of the wind or breath' from Greek *pneuma*, 'breath, wind'.

A **poem** is etymologically 'something created', from Greek *poein*, 'create, make', and developed metaphorically via 'literary work', to **poem**.

To **poeteeze** is to write poety.

A **pointillist** is a painter who creates separate dots of pure colour instead of mixed pigments; the pronunciation is PWAHN-tuhl-ist.

Polish comes from Latin *polire*, 'make smooth and shiny'.

Polite actually meant 'polished' or 'burnished' when it came into English.

Poltroon is a word for a mean-spirited, worthless wretch.

To **polylogize** is to talk excessively.

Poplin may stand for the 'Pope's linen'.

Popular goes back to Latin *populous*, 'people'.

Porcelain is from Italian *porcellana*, 'cowrie shell', and it led to its being the name for chinaware with comparable translucency and hardness.

Porcupine comes from Latin *porcus*, 'pig', and *spina*, 'thorn'.

Pore comes from a Greek word meaning 'passage'.

A **portent** is that which portends or foretells something momentous.

A **porter**, from Latin '*porta gate*', is one who is in charge of a door or gate.

Portfolio comes from Italian for 'carry' and 'sheets or leaves of paper'.

Post-cenal means after-dinner.

A **potato** is also a hole in a sock through which flesh protrudes.

POTUS is an abbreviation for President of the United States.

Poultry is derived from Latin *pullus*, 'young animal' or 'chicken'; a **pullet** is a young hen between the ages of chicken and mature fowl.

Potpourri comes from French *pot pourri*, which literally means 'rotten pot' and was first a stew made of different kinds of meat.

Pragmatic applies when the question is the planning with respect to these affairs; **practical** is anything that can be done and is worth doing well while **practicable**—worthwhile or not.

Praise first meant 'set a price on, attach a value to'.

Preach comes from the Latin elements *prae*, 'before', and *dicare*, 'declare'.

A **précis** is a concise or abridged statement, a summary, an abstract.

Precise comes from Latin elements meaning *prae*, 'in advance', and *caedere*, 'to cut'.

Predict (Latin *prae*, *pre-*, and *dicere*, 'say') first was 'mention previously in speech or writing'.

Pre-empt is from Latin elements meaning in advance and 'buy'.

Pregnant probably comes from *prae*, 'before', and *gnasci*, 'be born'.

Premiere is 'first night' in French.

Premium first meant 'prize, reward'.

Prerogative comes from Latin *praerogare*, 'ask before others', and came to mean 'right to precedence, privilege'.

Presbycusis (or **prebyacusis**) is loss of hearing as part of the aging process.

Pre-school is the adjective meaning 'before school'.

President comes from Latin *stems* meaning 'sit before'.

Presumptuous means 'assuming an unwarranted, unauthorized responsibility'.

A **preterist** lives in the past and is constantly nostalgic.

Pribble is vain chatter.

Pronoun is from *pro-*, 'on behalf of' and *nomen*, 'name'.

Pronounce is *pro-*, 'forth, out', and *nunhare*, 'announce'.

Proper first meant 'inherent, intrinsic'.

Property and propriety are doublets, sharing the ancestor, Latin *proprietas*, 'ownership', a derivative of *proprius*.

The **proscenium** is the part of the theatre space between the curtain or drop-scene and the orchestra, often including the curtain itself.

Prose is from Latin *prosa*, 'straight-forward discourse'.

Protect comes from Latin *pro*, 'in front, ' and *tegere*, 'cover'.

Protégé is from Latin meaning 'protect' and it means 'person under protection or patronage of another'.

A **proselyte** is etymologically someone who 'comes to' a new religion, from Greek *proseluthos*, 'person who comes to a place'.

Proto-language is any once-spoken language from which daughter languages descend.

A **protreptic** is a pep talk or exhortation; as an adjective, it is another word for 'instructive'.

Proud comes from Latin *prodesse*, 'be good', 'be of value'.

Proverb, from *pro-*, 'forth,' and *verbum*, 'word' is a saying put forth as a familiar truth; **Proveriology** is a set of proverbs or proverbs as a field of study.

Provide first meant 'foresee', literally, 'look ahead' (Latin *pro-* and *videre*).

Psalm comes from Greek *psalmos*, 'song sung to harp music'.

Psilology is a love of trivial or vacuous talk.

Psychopathy first meant 'mental illness'.

Psychurgy is mental energy.

To **publish** something is etymologically to 'make it public' from Latin *publicare*, 'make public'.

Puddingtime is another word for dinnertime.

Pugnacious (eager to fight) originated in Latin *pugnus*, 'fist'.

Punctual (from Latin *punctum*, 'point') can mean 'pertaining to punctuation' or 'of or relating to a point in space'.

Pundit is from Sankrit *pandito*, 'learned, conversant with or scholar'.

Latin *punier*, was derived from *poena*, 'penalty, punishment' and gave us **punish**.

Purgatory is from Latin *purgatories*, 'purifying', and it first meant a place or condition of spiritual cleansing.

Purport is normally applied to things, not people.

A word's **purpose** is its effect, import, or meaning.

Put is one of the most common English verbs, but its origins are uncertain; the golfing term **putt** (from Scottish) is essentially **putt**, just differentiated in spelling and pronunciation.

Pyrology is the science of fire or heat.

Pysmatic is always asking questions.

Q

Quacksalver, one who quacks, 'boasts' the virtues of salves and ointments.

Quadrangle is from Latin for 'four angles/corners' or 'square (thing)'.

Quag is a marshy or boggy spot, especially covered with turf that gives way when walked upon, and **quagmire** first meant the same thing.

Quaint first described a person as being 'clever, ingenious' and once meant 'elegant, graceful, subtle'.

Qualify first meant 'to describe (something) in a particular way'.

Qualitative refers to the characteristics or properties of quality and **quantitative** refers to the measure of something.

Quality comes from Latin *quails*, 'of what sort'.

Quandary may come from Latin *quando*, 'when'.

Quarantine comes from Italian *quaranta*, 'forty'—the number of days a ship was kept outside port if the ship's people had a contagious disease.

Quarterpace is a staircase landing at which the flights form a right angle.

Quench first meant 'extinguish a fire or light'.

To be **querulous** is to be inclined to complain.

In **quicksand, quick** means 'alive' as opposed to weight-bearing sand.

Quip originally was a sarcastic or sharp remark—or a curious or odd action.

Quirk was first a verb meaning 'move jerkily'.

Quits in 'call it quits' probably comes from a scribe's shortening of the medieval Latin *quittus*, 'discharged'.

Quixotic means 'visionary' or 'naively idealistic'.

Quiz has a meaning 'eccentric or odd person' and also 'a practical joke; hoax'.

Quizzism is the practice of questioning or quizzing.

Quodammodotative is a 'thing that exists in a certain way' (or an adjective meaning such).

Quop means 'to throb with pain'.

QWERTY keyboards are named for the first six letters of the upper keyboard.

R

Rabbi means 'my master' in Hebrew.

Rabid and **rabies** comes from Latin *rabere*, 'be mad'.

A **raconteur** or **raconteuse** is a teller of anecdotes, from French *raconter*, 'relate'.

Radiators have a misleading name, as they actually work by convecting heat, not radiating it.

Raj is Hindi for 'reign'.

Ramification is a subdivision of a complex.

Randy, from Scottish, means 'lewd, lecherous' or 'coarse, rude'.

A bookcase with a double face, as in a library, is a **range**.

Ransack is from Old Norse *rannsaka*, 'to search for stolen goods'.

The 'seam' of the tongue is the **raphe**.

Rapport, from French *rapporter*, 'bring back' is based on the notion of 'return'.

Rare as in steak is an alteration of rear/rere, 'half-cooked'.

Rate comes from Latin *rata*, 'calculated, fixed'.

Ratio is from Latin, literally 'reckoning'.

Ratiocinate is a fancy word for 'to reason'.

Ration is from Latin *ratio*, 'calculation, computation,' and in the Middle Ages took on the sense of 'amount of provisions allotted to a soldier'.

Rawky means 'foggy, damp, and cold'.

To **rax** is to stretch oneself after sleep.

A **ream** used to be 480 sheets of paper and now it is 500.

Rebellion is open resistance to a government or authority; **revolution** is a **rebellion** that succeeds in overthrowing the government and establishing a new one.

To **receive** something is etymologically to 'take it back,' from Latin *recipere*, 'regain'.

To **recense** is to review or revise a text; scholarly editorial revision is **recension**.

Recent is from Latin *recens*, 'fresh, new'.

A recipe collection is a **receptary**.

Recondite, 'abstruse, obscure' means etymologically 'hidden'.

Recoup first meant 'cut short, interrupt'.

Recourse refers to turning to someone or something for help; **resort** is something you turn to after all other options have failed (and as a verb means to have **recourse**).

Recrement is any superfluous or useless part of a substance.

Rectalgia or **proctalgia** is a pain in the behind.

Rectify is based on Latin *rectus*, 'right, straight'.

Rectigrade describes walking in a straight line.

Redamation is loving in return.

Redeem first meant 'buy back' and one of its Latin elements is *emere*, 'buy'.

Reebok is the Dutch name for a speedy South African antelope.

Refer comes from Latin meaning 'carry back' and a **referee** is a person to whom a matter or question is 'carried back' for a decision.

Refulgent is shining with or reflecting a brilliant light.

Regard is from French *regarder*, 'look back at, keep one's eyes on'.

Regent is from Latin *regere*, 'rule'.

Reiki is Japanese for 'universal life energy'.

A **rein** is etymologically something that 'retains'.

Relegate can mean 'send a person into exile'.

Relevant means 'worthy of raising in the context of discussion', **pertinent** means 'applicable to the point at issue'.

Religion comes from a Latin word meaning 'reverence' and originally meant a life under monastic vows.

A **reliquary** is a small receptacle for relics.

Relish first meant 'odour, scent', then 'taste, flavour'.

Remark is from an intensified French word *marquer*, 'observe, notice', i.e., 'making a verbal observation'.

Remote is from latin *remotes*, the past participle of *removere*, 'remove'.

Rendezvous is French for 'present yourselves'.

A **reprographer** is a person who makes copies of documents.

To **reprove** is to reject or express disapproval of something.

Republic comes from Latin *res*, 'affair or thing', and public,.

Repugn means 'to strive against' or 'be contradictory or inconsistent,' giving us **repugnant**.

Require includes the Latin element *quaerere*, 'ask, seek'.

Roast originally meant 'cook before a fire' before it meant 'cook in an oven'.

Rob goes back to Germanic *roub*, 'to break'.

Robot derives from Czech *robota*, 'forced labor'.

A **robot** is a fully mechanical conscience-less device; an **android** is an autonomous humanlike **robot**.

Rom-com means 'romantic comedy'.

A long string of beads for prayer is a **rosary**; a short string is a **chaplet**.
Roseate can mean rose-coloured, rose-scented, or just plain rosy.
A **rough-rider** breaks in horses.
Ruckus is probably a blend of rumpus and ruction.
Rudiment is from Latin *rudis*, 'unlearned, untrained,' and is patterned on *elementum*, 'element'.
A continuous low drumbeat is a **ruffle**, a continuous even drumbeat is a **tattoo**, a continuous loud drumbeat is a **drumroll**.
To **rump** is to snub, give the cold shoulder.
Rainwater not absorbed by the earth is **run-off**.
Rx comes from Latin, with the R standing for 'take this' and x for Jupiter, the Roman god of medicine.

S

Safe once referred to a box or cupboard where provisions were kept.
Saga is Old Norse for 'narrative'.
Saint comes from Latin *sanctus*, 'holy'.
Salad is a shortened version of Latin *herba salata*, 'salted vegetables' (from Latin *sal*, 'salt').
Salami is the plural of salame, 'salt pork', a derivative of the Italian verb *salare*, 'salt'.
Salsa is Spanish and Italian for 'sauce'.
Sausage's name goes back to Latin *salsus*, 'salted' while **wurest** is from Latin *veriere*, 'roll, turn', a reference to its cylinder shape.
Scalp originally meant 'top of the head, cranium'.
Scalpel comes from Latin *scalprum*, 'chisel'.
To **scamander** is to wander about or meander.
To **scarp** is to slope, cut a steep face.
Scat is slang for whiskey.
Schedule goes back to Greek *skhede*, for 'leaf of papyrus,' and started

out meaning a ticket or brief note.

Schemozzle or **shemozzle** is a muddle or complication.

Sciatic in **sciatic** nerve is from Greek, meaning 'relating to the hips, hip joints'.

Scibility is the power of knowing.

Science is from Latin *scientia*, 'knowledge', (from *scire*, 'know'), *sciental* is 'concerning or having knowledge'.

A curved sword is a **scimitar**.

Scissors comes from *cisorium*, 'cutting instrument'; **shears** describes a large implement (over 6 inches of blade) and **scissors** describes a smaller one.

Shittle means unstable, inconstant.

Shod means 'wearing shoes'.

Shore is the general word for an edge of land directly bordering a body of water; **coast** is limited to land along a sea or ocean.

Shruff is refuse wood or other material.

The bars of a gate are often called **shuttles**.

Sialoquent pertains to someone who is spitting while speaking.

Sibling originally meant 'relative', not specifically a brother or sister.

Sibship is a relationship between siblings.

A **siscative** is a substance causing drying, especially when mixed with oil paint, etc.

Sideburns were first called burnsides, named for Civil War general Ambrose Burnside.

Sidewalk's original meaning was 'a stroll' and then 'a path running parallel to a main one'.

A **sight** is a measurement or observation taken with an optical device.

The **sight** is the area enclosed by a picture frame.

Signature is from Latin *signatura*, 'sign manual'.

Silkworms are not worms; they are caterpillars.

Simmer means 'be at a heat just below the boiling point'.

Simple means 'plain, uncomplicated'.

Simplistic means 'characterized by a forced, unwarranted simplicity'.

Sinister comes from Latin, 'to the left'—as left was associated with bad omens.

Sipid—of pleasing taste, flavour, or character—is the opposite of **insipid**.

Sir is a short form of **sire**, which originally came from Latin *senior*.

Skinny first meant 'pertaining to or affecting the **skin**'.

Skirmish is derived from Italian *scaramuccia*; the whirr of birds in flight is **skirr**.

A **skite** is a contemptible person.

Skullduggery is from Scottish *skulduddery*, 'unchaste behaviour'.

Sky comes from Old Norse *sky* meaning 'cloud' and at first referred only to clouds.

Sky-hook means 'wishful thinking'.

Slacks (as in pants) probably comes from Latin *laxus*, 'loose'.

Slaughter is from Old Norse meaning 'butcher's meat'.

Sleek is a variant form of slick.

Sleeveless once meant 'paltry, petty, frivolous'.

Soufflé, French for 'puffed up,' comes from Latin *subflare*, 'to puff or blow up from below', and also describes types of puffing, like breathing and inflating things with air and a murmuring breathing sound.

Soup is from French *soupe* and maybe Latin *suppa* (from *suppare*, 'soak'); **soup** originally denoted a piece of bread soaked in liquid, then broth poured onto bread.

A **sour** is a mixed drink consisting of whisky, brandy, or gin (etc.), lemon or lime juice—hence the name, and sugar.

South seems to come from the Germanic root *sunth/sunthaz*, 'sunny'.

Sozzled is a word meaning 'intoxicated'.

Spam, as in email, gets its name from the Monty Python sketch where the word is repeated many times.

Span was originally the distance between the tip of the thumb and tip of the little finger.

Spasm and **spastic** derive from Greek *span*, 'draw, pull'.

Spay is a shortening of a French word meaning 'cut with a sword'.

Specialization refers to the process of becoming specialized; **specialty** refers to a special pursuit, occupation, or product.

Specious means 'seeming to be correct or logical'.

Spellbind is 'bind with a spell'.

Spharistike (Greek for 'let's')was the original name for lawn tennis.

Sphere comes from Greek *sphaira*, 'ball'

A synonym for 'to appropriate' is **spheterize**.

A **spinosity** is a rude remark.

Spinster first pertained to a woman who spun cotton, wool, etc., for a living or one who had spun herself a set of body, table, and bed linen—and later was used as a legal designation for an unmarried woman. The activity or product of making fibre into yarn is **spinstry**.

Spissated is a synonym for thickened.

Something's **spissitude** is its density or thickness.

Spite is from French *despit*, 'ill will, scorn,' from Latin *despicere*, 'look down on'.

Spizzerinctum is personal drive or motivation.

Splash and spatter are combined into **splatter**.

Splenative is a synonym for irritable.

Splendid is from Latin *splendere*, 'shine'.

A six-ounce bottle of a beverage, like Champagne, is a **split**.

Spondulicks is slang for 'cash, money'.

Sponge is from Latin *spongia* and Greek *sphoggos*, 'water growth'.

Spongeous means 'having holes'.

A **squadron** is etymologically a 'square' and the sense of 'military group' comes from an earlier 'square formation of troops'; the word was borrowed from Italian *squadrone*, from Latin *quadrare*, 'square'.

To dirty something through handling is to **squage**.

Squirrel comes from Greek *skiouros*, from *skia*, 'shadow,' and *oura*, 'tail'.

Stage derives from Latin *stare*, 'stand'.

Stagnate comes from Latin *stagnum*, 'pool'; a stagnant pool is a **stagnum**.

In Old English, **stair** meant a whole flight of steps, not a single one.

Stake, 'post' comes from a Germanic base meaning 'pierce, prick'.

To **stammer** is to etymologically be 'impeded' in speech.

Stampede is from Mexican Spanish *estampida*, 'crash, uproar'.

Sundae is an alteration of Sunday—either because leftover ice cream was sold on Sunday or the dish was only served on that day.

Supernal means 'celestial, heavenly'.

Supplosion is stamping the feet in disapproval.

Supply is from Latin *supplere*, 'complete, fill up'.

Support is from Latin *supportare*, 'bring, carry, convey'.

Suppose seems to come from Latin *sup ponere*, 'put under'.

To **surbate** is to tire the feet with excessive walking.

A **surrogate** is etymologically someone who has been 'asked' to take the place of another, from Latin *subrogare*, 'nominate an alternative candidate'.

Sushi in Japanese means 'it is sour'; the *su* in sushi means 'vinegar' and the one ingredient common to all sushi is vinegared rice.

Sutile means 'made by sewing'.

Swasivious means 'agreeably persuasive'.

Swastika means 'benediction or well being' and was originally a good-luck sign.

Sweetmeat is made from fruit and **sweetbread** is made from meat (and is not sweet).

Swerve is related to middle Dutch *swerven*, 'to stray'.

A **sylloge** is a collection or summary.

Symmetry is formed from *sym-* and *metron*, 'measure', and symmetrical is patterned after geometrical.

Synapse is Greek for 'clasp together'.

Synergy can mean 'the whole is greater than the sum of the parts'.

Synesthesia is the comingling of the five senses.

Syngesophobia is dislike or fear of relatives.

Syndrome is from Greek elements meaning 'run together' and is a group of **symptoms**; **synopsis** literally means 'seeing together'.

A **synodite** is a travelling companion.

Syringes get their name for the cylindrical shape, from Greek *surigx*, 'pipe'.

T

The flap of a shoe is the **tab**.

Table tennis is often called by its trademarked name, **Ping-Pong**.

A **tableau** is a graphic or vivid description tablet. It is from Old French *tablete*, from a diminutive of Latin *tabula*, 'list, plank, **tablet**'.

Tacit means 'unspoken, silent' or 'implied, inferred'.

Tachygraphy is the art or practice of quick writing, as shorthand.

Taciturn means habitually untalkative.

Tactic is etymologically 'arrangement, setting in order,' from Greek *tassein*, 'put in order' or 'formation', 'arrange in battle formation'.

Tactical comes from Greek *taktikos/taktos*, 'arranged, ordered'.

Tactual means 'arising from or due to touch' and **tactile** means 'capable of, allows for being touched'.

Tae-bo is Korean for 'leg boxing'.

A **tale** is etymologically something that is 'told'.

Talisman is derived from Greek *telesmon*, 'consecrated object'.

Contact at a single point is a **tangent**.

Tangible means literally 'touchable,' from Latin *tangere*, 'touch'—it is literally some thing that can be touched but also can be a feeling so strong that it seems 'touchable'.

A **tanling** is a person tanned by the sun.

Tapestry is based on French *tapis*, 'carpet'.

Taratantara is pretentious talk.

The sound of a bugle or trumpet can be called **taratantara**.

Tardy is from Latin *tardus*, 'slow'.

Tat are worthless articles.

The edge of a handkerchief is the **tat**.

Tax is from Latin *taxare*, 'censure, charge, or compute'.

Taxi is an abbreviation of taximeter and taxicab.

The fare device in **taxis** is the **taximeter**.

Tazzled is another word for entangled.

Technology, from Greek *tekhnologia* and its root *tekhne*, 'art or craft,' meant 'systematic treatment'—as a study of the arts.

Teenful means troublesome or irritating.

Teetotal is total plus 'tee' as an emphatic extension (reproducing the first letter) thereby meaning 'total total' (reduplication) in reference to total abstinence, first used to refer to this by Richard Turner in a speech in 1833.

Telephone is from Greek *tele*, 'afar,' and *phone*, 'sound, voice,' and it was first called the speaker **telegraph**.

Television literally means 'see at a distance'.

Tenant comes from Latin *tenere*, 'to hold'.

Tenderloin is the most tender cut of meat—in beef, from below the short ribs and made up of the psoas muscle.

Tenebrous means gloomy or dark.

Tennis is from French *tenez*, 'take, receive,' which was originally called out by the server to the opponent.

A **tennist** is one who plays tennis.

Tense is from Latin *tendere*, 'stretch'.

Tension was first a medical term for the condition of being physically strained.

Tepid is from Latin *tepere*, 'be warm'.

Terrain was once the exercise training ground for horses at a riding school.

A **terran** is an earth inhabitant.

The word **terrapin** comes from the Algonquin *toarebe* or *turupem*, meaning 'little turtle'.

The ring on an animal collar for attaching a leash is the **terret**.

A **tete-a-tete** is an S-shaped sofa on 'which two people can sit face to face'.

Than is ultimately the same word as **then** and the two were used interchangeably until the end of the seventeenth century.

A hollow or rut across a road is colloquially called '**thank-you-ma'am**'.

Thin denotes etymologically 'stretched'.

In Old English, **thing** meant 'court, assembly, council'.

Thirty, written 30, indicates the end of a story in journalism, first used in Morse Code for its distinctive.

Thousand is an ancient noun originally meaning 'several hundreds'.

Throne is from Greek *thronos*, 'elevated seat'.

Thumb was *thuma*, 'thick, swollen,' in Old English.

Etymologically, **thunder** is 'noise,' from the Indo-European *ton/tn*, 'resound'.

Thursday is Thor's Day, the Germanic god of thunder (*thunor*).

Tight as in 'sleep tight' may be from the sense 'soundly, roundly' of the 1700s.

Timeful is another word for seasonable or timely.

Tinct is a poetic term for 'colour' or 'colouring matter'; **tint** is an alteration of **tinct**, 'to colour'.

Titillate is from Latin *titillare*, 'to tickle'.

A **tittynope** is a small quantity of anything left over.

Tizzy is possibly a blend of tipsy and dizzy.

Tobacco comes from the Carib word *tubaco* which meant the reed pipes in which the natives smoked the dried leaves—but it came to represent the leaves and then the **tobacco** plant.

U

Ugly is from Old Norse *uggligr*, 'be feared,' from *ugga*, 'feel or fill with dread'.

Ulterior is from a Latin word literally meaning 'further, more distant'.

Ultramontane means 'beyond the mountains'.

Ultrasound or **ultrasonography** work on the principle that sound is reflected at different speeds by tissues or substances of different densities.

An **umberment** is a multitude.

Umbilical is from Latin *umbilicus*, 'navel'.

Umbra is the darkest part of a shadow.

Uncle is From Latin *avunculus*, 'mother's brother, maternal uncle'.

Underprivileged first meant lacking some legal right(s).

Universe denotes etymologically 'turned into one' or 'indivisible, whole,' from Latin *universus* (*unus*, 'one,' and *versus/vertere*, 'turn').

Unkempt variant of unkembed, from *kemb*, 'comb'.

Upset first meant 'set up; raise, erect'.

Upstage in theatre is 'towards the rear of the stage' and **downstage** is 'towards the audience'; **stage left** and right are left and right as the audience views the stage.

Uranium is named for Ouranos, ancient sky god of Greek mythology.

Uranomania is the delusion that one is descended from heaven.

Urban is from Latin *urbs*, 'city'.

Urban refers to a city; **urbane** means polished and smooth, as in a person's demeanour.

Usher was originally a term for a door-keeper.

Usual means etymologically that which is commonly 'used' or employed or commonly obtained—from Latin *usualis*.

Uterus is from Latin *uterus*, 'belly, womb'.

Utter first meant 'outer, outward'.

Uxorial is 'pertaining to a wife' and **uxorious** is 'overly fond of one's wife'.

V

Vacant is from Latin *vacare*, 'be empty'.

Vacation is a word coming from Latin *vacation/vacatio*, from *vacare*, to be 'free, empty; to be at leisure', and around 1395, this term entered Old English, meaning 'rest and freedom from any activity'.

A **valetudinarian** is someone who is unnecessarily anxious about their health.

Valid and **value** come from Latin *valere*, 'be strong'.

Vamoose comes from Spanish *vamos*, 'let as go'.

Van is a shortening of caravan.

Vanish is from Latin *evanescere*, 'die away'.

Vanquish comes from Latin *vincere*, 'conquer'.

Vapour is from Latin *vapour*, 'heat, steam'.

Vase is Latin *vas*, 'vessel'.

Vein is from Latin *vena*, 'blood vessel'.

Velcro gets its name from French *vel(ours) cro(che)*, 'hooked velvet'.

Vend is from Latin *vendere*, 'sell'.

Sudden or unexpected changes in life are **vicissitudes**.

Victual is from Latin *viciualia*, 'provisions' — and is properly pronounced VIH-tuhl.

Vie is a shortened version of *envie*, 'make a challenge'.

View is etymologically something 'seen'.

The part you look through on a camera is the **viewfinder**.

To **vilify** is to say defamatory things about someone.

Vincible means conquerable.

Vinegar is from French *vyn egre*, based on Latin *vinum*, 'wine', and *acer*, 'sour'.

Viscerotonic is having a sociable, easy going, comfort-seeking personality.

Visnomy is a person's face or expression, especially as an indication of character and mind.

Vital is from Latin *vitalis* and *vita*, 'life'.

Vitiate is 'to make imperfect; spoil'.

Vitreous is from Latin *vitrum*, 'glass', and *vitreus*, 'clear, transparent'.

To **vituperate** is to verbally abuse; **vituperation** implies fluent and sustained abuse.

The adjective form for calf is **vituline**.

Vocabular means 'of or pertaining to words'.

Voice is from Latin *vox*, 'voice'.

The **voicebox** is the **larynx**.

Void means empty; **devoid** means empty, but empty only after something has been taken away.

A **voluptuary** is one totally into luxury and sensual pleasure.

Votal means 'associated with or having the nature of a vow'.

Voodoo derives from West African *vodu*, 'demon'.

Vouch originally meant 'call as a witness'.

Voyeur is French for 'one who sees'.

Vulgate is accepted everyday speech.

Vulnerable is from Latin *vulnus*, 'wound'.

To **vum** is to swear or vow.

Wabbit means 'tired out, exhausted'.

Waist is etymologically 'girth to which one has grown'.

Wan can mean 'bland' or 'uninterested'.

Wane suggests the fading or weakening of something good or impressive.

To **wantonize** is to flirt or dally with.

A **wap** is a piece of string wrapped around something.

A **watermelon** is really a berry and it was first written as two words.

Wax (verb) is from Old English *weaxan*, 'to become' or 'to grow'.

A **waypoint** is a stopping place on a journey.

The **wayside** is the edge of a road.

The original meaning of **wayward** was 'turning away' or 'turned away'.

If one is good at not getting lost, then one is **waywise**.

Weak is from a Germanic base meaning 'give way, yield'.

Weigh first meant 'carry, lift, bear, raise up'.

Welcome first referred to a person whose arrival was desirable or pleasing.

Well is an adverb to describe an activity; **good** is an adjective to describe a condition or state.

Wheel is etymologically something that 'goes around'.

Whelk is a euphemism for pimple.

Another word for trinket is **whim-wham**.

Whisper is from a base which imitated a hissing sound.

Wicked is probably based on Old English *wicca*, 'witch'.

Wife originally meant simply 'woman' but by Old English it was 'married woman'.

Willy-nilly is a contraction of 'will I, nill I'.

Wink is the closing of the eyes for sleep.

Workaholic was coined in the late 1960s by Wayne Oates, an American pastoral counsellor, from work + a(lco)holic.

To **wrangle** can mean 'to scream with passion'.

The **wrist** of the foot is the instep or ankle.

All Western Indo-European languages except English derive the verb for 'to write' from Latin *scribere*; English **write** comes from Old

English *writan*, meaning 'form letters by carving'.
Wrong originally meant 'crooked, twisted, bent'.

X

X is the horizontal axis and **y** is the vertical.
In mathematics, there are three quantities: **X, Y,** and **Z**.
Xanthodontous is having yellow teeth.
A guidebook for visitors is a **xenagogy**.
Xenolochial means hospitable to strangers.
Xeres is another word for sherry.
X-height is the height of lower-case letters.
The initial letter X in **Xmas** (Christmas) the is letter *chi* of Khristos 'Christ'.
X-ray puzzled by his discovery, Roentgen named it.
XXX and **000** added at the end of a letter for kisses and hugs probably originated in the Middle Ages when illiterate people would sign an X for their name and then kiss the paper as a sign of good faith.

Y

Year's root sense is 'what passes'.
Yemeles means 'careless, negligent'.
Yen as in the currency of Japan comes from the Chinese word *yuan*, meaning 'round thing' or 'dollar'.
A **yesterfang** is something that was caught or taken yesterday.
Yestreen is yesterday evening.
Yield first meant 'payment'.

Z

Zen is from Sanskrit *dhyana*, 'meditation', from a Proto-Indo-European root meaning 'to observe, see'.

Zephyr is a breeze from the west or gentle breeze, based on the ancient Greek name for the west wind.

Zest can be traced back only to French *zeste*, 'orange or lemon peel'.

Zetetic means 'asking, questioning'.

A **zig** or a **zag** is one leg of a zigzag.

A **ziggurat** is a tower in the form of a terraced pyramid.

Zimbabwe, 'walled grave,' was formerly Rhodesia.

Ziraleet is a sudden expression of joy, an exultation.

Zoilism is destructive or carping criticism.

Zorro means 'fox' in Spanish.

Zwieback means 'twice baked,' as it is a baked biscuit that is sliced and toasted.

A **zythepsary** is a brewhouse.